BROKEN TOGETHER HEALED

A JOURNEY THROUGH RESILIENCE AND RESTORATION

RICHARD AND JENNIFER KINARD

Copyright © 2025 Richard and Jennifer Kinard

All rights reserved. No part of this publication may be reproduced, distributed, or transmitted in any form or by any means, including photocopying, recording, or other electronic or mechanical methods, without the prior written permission of the publisher, except in the case of brief quotations embodied in critical reviews and certain other noncommercial uses permitted by copyright law. For permission requests, write to the publisher, addressed "Attention: Permissions Coordinator," at the address below.

Print ISBN: 979-8-9881065-6-2
eBook ISBN: 979-8-9881065-7-9

Published By My Peace of Happy

Printed in the United States of America

For permission requests, please email the publisher with the subject line as "Attention: Permissions Coordinator"
to the email address below:
Info@Opportunepublishing.com

DEDICATION

To our parents —Solomon & Phyllis Kinard, Dennis & Veronica Philbert —For being strong role models and being the parents God gave us not to know what was ahead.

ACKNOWLEDGMENTS

God, Our Father

Our Children:
Nya Love
Mya Kinard
Jeremiah Kinard

Our Coach, Jamie Watkins

Editor, Riel Felice

Publisher, Shanley Simpson

Dr. Pastor, Emeritus Magdalen Shelton

Pastor Leslie Christie

Our Mentor: Couples
Reuben and Lorraine Thompson
Kevin and Victoria Dickerson

"Family and Friends"

CONTENTS

Introduction 13

Chapter 1
Before Addiction Took Hold 17

Chapter 2
The Slippery Slope: The Search of What Lies Beyond 29

Chapter 3
Hitting Rock Bottom 53

Chapter 4
A Moment of Clarity 61

Chapter 5
Seeking Help Together 71

Chapter 6
Early Days of Recovery 85

Chapter 7
Rebuilding Trust 97

Chapter 8
The Role of God, Counseling and Therapy 107

Chapter 9
Staying Sober, Staying Strong 115

Chapter 10
Rediscovering Love and Intimacy..*123*

Chapter 11
Our New Life Together..*131*

Chapter 12
You Are Not Alone..*137*

Chapter 13
Finding Faith and Purpose in Recovery.......................................*143*

Chapter 14
Advice for Couples..*153*

Conclusion..*159*

Conclusion..*163*

INTRODUCTION

Life is a journey, and things happen that often break us in ways we never imagined. Sometimes it's an immediate hit of life challenges that may cause things to shatter; other times, it feels like life is moving in slow motion while hope, trust or dreams are falling apart. For us, the breaking came through the monster of addiction and the strain and roller-coaster ride it placed on our marriage, our faith, our mental states, our emotions and our very identities. It left us shattered and broken, unsure of how to move forward or if we even could.

But this is not a story about staying broken. It's about our journey of finding the pieces, trusting God, being in the process, and holding on to what's left in hopes that we can have a stronger and more meaningful marriage than before. This is a story about unlocking resilience, healing and restoration — not only within us but also in our relationships and with God.

As you read this book, you'll journey with us through the highs, lows and very lows of recovery and rediscovery. Everyone gets to see the painful truths we had to confront, the small victories that gave us some hope and the lessons we learned along the way. As we ventured on this journey, we experienced first the searing pain of brokenness and the paths towards healing and rebuilding. We found that journeying through healing comes with pure honesty, being vulnerable and resilient, and an unyielding commitment to growth individually and as a couple. By no means was this journey easy, and we found that there was no way either of us could have gone through it without God.

We want this book to be a mirror and a roadmap for you. Whether you're dealing with your own brokenness or walking alongside someone else, our prayer is that you'll find hope, encouragement and practical wisdom for your own journey.

Healing doesn't happen overnight. It's messy, raw and often uncomfortable. But it's also transformative and deeply beautiful. We hope that when you read this book, you will allow God to open your hearts, hear the story, and see how God moved and is still moving. Every day is a lesson in understanding the things that you have to deal with, trusting God and trusting the process. We do know that every relationship is not the same, but every relationship could use God in it. We hope someone gets rescued from this overall journey of addiction and the added pain that comes with it. As you turn each page, we share our testimony and give reverence to the power of God and our love for each other, in hopes that those who may feel alone, scared, frustrated, undecided, hurt, angry and much more would grab hold to something in here that would give them the strength to get to the other side.

"Therefore let us [with privilege] approach the throne of grace [that is, the throne of God's gracious favor] with confidence and without fear, so that we may receive mercy [for our failures] and find [His amazing] grace to help in time of need [an appropriate blessing,

coming just at the right moment]." — Hebrews 4:16

Welcome to Broken TOGETHER Healed: A Journey Through Resilience and Restoration.

Let's begin the journey!

BROKEN *TOGETHER* HEALED

CHAPTER 1

BEFORE ADDICTION TOOK HOLD

Richard: Life before addiction, early signs and what led to substance abuse

Hi. It's not by coincidence you are reading this book. I believe that the Holy Spirit led you this way. So since you are here, allow me to introduce myself. My name is Richard Kinard, I'm 57 years old and I was born in Brooklyn, New York. I had a normal childhood, no major trauma. I was never molested, no physical or emotional abuse.

I was just a curious boy; I was about seven or eight years old when my curiosity sat in. You know back in the '70s, my parents would send me to the store to buy beer and cigarettes with no ID. Sometimes I would sneak and drink some of my father's beer and smoke some of my mother's cigarettes. My parents weren't bad parents; I just wanted to try the beer and cigarettes, and so I did. My parents would take me to church. My father's father was a preacher, and my mother's family were God-fearing people. The church my mother grew up in would catch the Holy Ghost all the time.

I spent more time at my father's church; they didn't shout as much there. Both sides of my family were people of faith, but as I said, this was the early '70s, and there were house parties and a lot of family gatherings. These house parties and family gatherings would have a lot of drinking happening, so I knew and saw things. This is not to put the blame on anyone — it was fun for me. I enjoyed my childhood.

So we moved around a lot, and when I was about 11 years old, here came curiosity. It was the first time I tried to get high. I found some marijuana roaches in my older brother's dresser drawer, and I tried it, but nothing happened.

Looking back at that now, it seems like God was trying to protect me from what was to come.

After a few years passed, I was in junior high school. A couple of friends and I decided to smoke some weed this time. It was not a small roach, but it was a whole joint, not like the roaches I found in my brother's drawer and tried to get high with. But I still didn't feel the effects of the whole joint. You would have thought I would have stopped right there. My curiosity just kept me seeking to get high — until this one day, while smoking in the hallway what we called a blunt back in the day, I finally felt the effects of the weed. Man, that night, I was so paranoid. I was talking crazy; everything I said made no sense at all.

I wish I didn't get high at all, but it was too late. The curiosity from my childhood opened Pandora's box, and I was hooked on getting high.

Then, in high school, I tried cocaine for the first time. My world became full of alcohol and drugs. To be honest, though, I preferred getting high over getting drunk; alcohol really wasn't my problem. With that being said, the crack epidemic surfaced in 1986, and this was a game changer. I was about 18 years old, and I would mix marijuana and crack. I'd smoke it thinking that if I smoked it that way, I wouldn't get hooked on the glass pipe. YEAH, RIGHT! Remember, I was a kid. Curiosity continued kicking in; from 18 to about 26, I was stuck in the world of smoking crack. My life was slipping further and further into darkness, man. There were many nights I would cry out to God to help me, promising not to get high no more. Well, you could only imagine how that went.

Now, I lost my identity and couldn't find myself. If only I'd never been curious and experimented with drugs — I used to tell myself that all the time. All I had at this time in my life was prayer and a few scriptures. As the days passed, I kept fighting to regain my life back.

This is until God sent me, my rib, my wife. She and I met at church. Yeah, I said church. We really were good friends at first; my parents had a 1986 Grand Am, and I would drive that many times. On occasion, I would drop Jenny home after working together those days. We would talk about different things that we were going through. She didn't really know about my drug habit. That was something I didn't mention, but I had no intention of having a relationship with her anyway, so why would I?

It wasn't until I received a phone call from her that we decided to start dating.

The phone call went like this:

"Hey, Rich."

"Hi, Jen."

"Hey, Rich. Can I ask you something?"

"Sure."

"I heard someone likes me."

"Jen, let me stop you right there. You called me about another person. I think you really calling about me to ask if I like you."

Well, she said she did like me, and I liked her too. Jen hates when I tell this part of the story, but I love to tell it.

So then, we were dating. Things were great. We were spending a lot of time together, and God was starting to move in our relationship.

We were praying together, studying the Bible together and talking about God a lot. We sang in the choir together and we hung out at the church all the time, but my secret was still haunting me.

"Two are better than one, because they have a good return for their labor: If either of them falls down, one can help the other up. But pity anyone who falls and has no one to help them up." (Ecclesiastes 4: 9–10)

Time went on, and we developed a relationship.

Jenny got pregnant out of wedlock, and we were still dating. We knew it wasn't right in the eyes of God and of people, but we were happy. I know I was happy; I was going to be a father. Jenny was happy. Those were good times. So we decided that after Jenny gave birth to our first daughter, she would come and stay in our home. My parents did not want us to live together being that we weren't married, so at night, when it was time for us to go to bed, I had to go and stay at my brother's apartment next door. My mother and I would talk, and then I would talk to God. Regardless of what other people were thinking or what their opinions might've been, I didn't really listen to them. I remember God just telling me one night, "You know that she's a good woman, and she would be a great mother." I often heard men say, "You'll know she's the one if she reminds you of your mother." No, Jenny didn't remind me of my mother; she reminded me of my wife for the future. She would be my wife, not my mother. She would be a great mother to my children. I saw a mother for my children, not a mother for me. We got married on June 26, 1993, the beginning of our life together. We lived with my parents for a while.

My mother, who passed away, loved my wife. She loved Jenny. My wife would take care of my mother because my mother was sick; she had breast cancer and was bedridden. She couldn't even walk.

I remember one time my mother calling out to me, "Rich, come and wash me." I was so embarrassed.

I was like, "Mom, I'm ashamed."

Jenny said, "I'll do it."

My mother was like, "No, let him come do it."
Jenny was explaining to my mother, "He's embarrassed."

So, Jenny bathed my mother. She took care of my mother. I can go on and on with stories about my mother and how she felt towards Jen. The last days of me and my mother were great; we really got tight, and my mother was not concerned about me, but I thank God that she was able to see her granddaughter and her son get married. I'm not the youngest child, but I was the last one to get married, and she got to see that. I believe she was happy. Did losing my mother affect me? Not to the point where it made me go and get high like that. But there were days when I'd say, "I miss Mommy." I wish she could see who I am and what I became. Her prayers were answered. My mother prayed for me, and her prayers were answered.

"Start children off on the way they should go, and even when they are old they will not turn from it." — Proverbs 22:6 NIV

Jennifer: How addiction crept into our marriage, and the early warning signs I missed or ignored

I now know that addiction silently creeps into relationships. Signs are easy to dismiss and overlook. I was born to Dennis and Veronica Philbert in Trinidad and Tobago; my parents decided to move to America, the land of the free. That's what we knew America to be, that rich place. Coming to America meant encountering changes upon changes. One of those changes was joining a new church and meeting new people. I never wanted to join the church my mother attended, but no child of Veronica tells her no, they're not doing something — much less not attending church or joining a church. So I joined the church, joined the choir, participated in the feeding program and much more. The food pantry is where I met my husband. We used to converse a lot, and we served together in that ministry and the music ministry.

I enjoyed spending time with him. He was tall, handsome, well-dressed and a good friend. I liked him a lot. We used to have long telephone conversations and even pray together. I don't know if it was cluelessness or just being naive, but I did not know he was smoking during those times. It was something other than what we discussed. I never smelled it on him. I didn't know; all I knew was that I was falling for this guy. I knew that he drank, but I still didn't know he was doing drugs. As I look back, tears flow from my eyes because I stopped to ask myself how stupid I could have been in all those conversations, all those late-night talks, and why I didn't see the signs. Why didn't I ask him a question? But I continued to date him. I used to spend money on us, and I gave him money too, but I was in love, and I believed he was the person for me.

My understanding of drugs at the time was dim. I have no clue how time went on, and in 1992, I became pregnant with our first child. He was still doing drugs, smoking and drinking, but I was still in the space of the unknown. I just don't know why I didn't allow myself to see it — and what if I'd realized it or known it? What would I have done by this time? I'd fallen in love with him and had his first child. I sure wasn't seeing drugs as a problem — or as a soon-to-be problem — in our lives. If I'm honest, I was 19 when I first met Richard. I didn't know about drugs and weed and whatever else he was engaged in. I just didn't see it, but after some time, I was just scared — scared to ask what was going on, scared to ask why he was always upset, scared to ask why he was always so moody. I didn't understand him. Before marrying him, I honestly can say that it's almost like I was in denial, like that wasn't happening. But it was happening, and I was just dumb or clueless.

I couldn't have been that dumb before I married him. Why didn't I decline? Why didn't I think? Why didn't I think that it could get worse? I don't know what I was thinking.

I honestly didn't know what else he was engaging himself in. I didn't know what was going to happen next.

Right before my eyes, things were changing. I'm not even sure if he was honest or if we were at a place of being open to sharing and talking about drugs, but when I started paying attention back then, he used to love to hang out and drink. Then, I noticed that he was making money but not keeping money, and we began to struggle financially. If I had to think and ask myself, *What were the early warning signs?*, it was the constant hanging out, the drinking, the munchies, the mood swings, the wanting to be intimate when *he* wanted to.

I thought it might have been girls, or maybe he did not want to come home to me. *Is something wrong with me?* I was not 100% sure of what was going on, and I kept asking myself, *Are you dumb?*

Eventually, it would all come crashing down and everything would be a lot clearer to me, but I still couldn't believe I'd missed all of those warning signs. What caused me to be so blind even though I knew that something was up? My focus wasn't even the drugs. Like I said, I thought it was some other female or something.

So, life went on as we continued to live in our old apartment. Our environment felt light, yet it felt like there was a heaviness that existed, almost like an elephant was in the room.

He was consistent with his hanging out, drinking and smoking. His friends and other people often called him out of the house. Back then, I felt as though they had no respect for marriage, and they used to say I was controlling. They had no idea of my reasons. Folks had no idea what I was living with, but all those things were his priority. He came home, maybe because he knew that I was going to be home — and guess what? He was right. I was always there when he came. Don't get me wrong — he put some of his money into the house, but not all of it. And it's like he didn't put it because whatever little he put, he took back from me.

When he came and wanted money from me, I would feel like I had to give it to him because if I didn't, it may have been a problem. His habit came first. I was not a factor. We weren't saving money; it was leaving the house as quickly as it came in. I had my biggest realization that something was wrong when I noticed things missing from my home, but I never spoke about it. He used to pawn and sell our kid's games and my DVDs. I didn't know initially, and there was nothing I could have done back then — at least that's how I felt. If I tried, there probably would have been an argument. If I had tried, maybe there would have been a fight, so I just surrendered each time. I didn't want to go back and forth with him. He even used to pawn my mother-in-law's ring. She left me her wedding ring when she passed, and he pawned it a few times, but eventually, I never got it back. I have no idea where that ring is. It's in some jewelry store, maybe on somebody else's finger.

The pawning and taking of things became a regular occurrence; it just became a habit of his. I remember him coming home one night so scared because of something that took place where he was hanging out, and all I could do was thank God for protecting him. I cried that night, asking God: "Please keep him home. Please make him stop going out. I don't know what to do anymore, God. I love him, and this is my husband. This is the man You gave to me. Please, God. This is a lot, and I don't know what to do. Please help."

I wanted to be the wife that God called me to be. I comforted my husband when he needed me. I cooked, I cleaned, I took care of our children. I did everything that I believed that I should have done as a wife, but it never seemed like it was enough. I often tried not to get emotional thinking about it or thinking about where he may be because deep down inside, I heard myself calling myself, *You fool. You don't get it. Say something, do something, anything.*

I heard myself talk back to myself and say, *What are you scared of? What are you concerned about? Do something.* All the signs were there: the mood swings, the hanging out, the late nights, the drunkenness probably coupled with the weed and the drugs, the munchies, the crankiness, all of it.

Jesus, thinking about the past, about all the behaviors I had to encounter, is painful. There was no way I could go through any of this without God. I didn't know I had the strength to go through, but I surely lacked faith. The many times I called on God, my faith was shaky.

It was all right there, and I missed it. What would have happened if I had caught it early enough?

There were moments I was called out of my name, cursed at, yelled at, with just no regard.

He was active at one time in church, and then he just stopped, so I just continued to attend and take our children.

I thought about talking to his family, saying something, doing something, but I wouldn't say anything because I didn't know what they would have thought about me. To be honest, I thought they knew something or at least knew more than me. I was scared. I was scared that I could lose him. I was scared that I could lose me. I was scared that something was going to happen to our family. I was scared that we wouldn't have a marriage anymore. All types of fears were flowing through me. My mom already didn't like him too much — well, she liked him at one point, but once I became pregnant, she didn't care much for him. She didn't like my choice, my decisions, so I couldn't run back home. I didn't want to show myself being defeated or prove my mother right at that time. So I stood and stuck it out because I believed that I was strong enough to handle it at that moment, and I believed that something had to give. This had to turn around. But I didn't know that there was more to come. I didn't know that there was more ahead of me.

Times that we spent on the phone while we were dating, praying and talking for long hours, we had no idea that we were cementing a foundation. We didn't even know what was coming into our lives ahead of us. We appreciate God for being the light in the midst of it all.

"But if we walk in the light, as he is in the light, we have fellowship with one another, and the blood of Jesus, his Son, purifies us from all sin." — 1 John 1:7 NIV

CHAPTER 2

THE SLIPPERY SLOPE: THE SEARCH FOR WHAT LIES BEYOND

Richard: How I fell deeper into addiction — triggers, temptations, and denial

My wife unwillingly became my enabler. She gave me what I needed when I asked for it. There were times when she tried to resist, and it would cause tension to arise. I didn't like the way I behaved back then, but I did not care to know what I was doing to the woman I knew truly loved me.

I knew that Jenny would always be home when I got home; there was no need for me to have another woman in my life. The drugs were the other woman at that time. I didn't like it — somebody who hasn't walked in my shoes would not even understand this — but I didn't care. I didn't care to look at what I was doing to the woman who I knew I truly loved. I wasn't able to express it; I was ashamed. After all, I felt like she wouldn't believe me because I'd lied so many times. My actions weren't the actions of a good husband, a good man, a God-fearing man that she would want. I felt she didn't want to hear it, but she was there. I knew she was there, and all the while, I was trying. I'd like to use this statement: "I would say to her, the Richard she was experiencing was the Richard deep inside of me — the old Richie who was using drugs, crying, 'Help, help. Don't you see me?' I felt like I was trapped in a bubble, and she couldn't hear me; she couldn't pull me out. I was inside of a soundproof room, and she couldn't hear the real Richard who was saying, 'Help me. H-help me. I can't get out; I'm trapped in here. Don't you see me?'"

When the other Richie was living in the world, causing havoc, putting his family in harm's way, people were threatening me. You know, if they couldn't get at me, they were threatening and saying they were going to get at my family. There were times when I thought I would have to kill someone to protect my family because I didn't know any other way, and my wife would step in and pay the debts for me. As I dealt with these various things, I kept slipping deeper and deeper into my addiction because I felt like doing it. I kept getting away with this. That Richie, the other Richie, became selfish, and I was like, *Well, I know she's going to take care of it. She's going to give it to me.* I also had a hustling lifestyle. If Jenny did not give me money, I knew how to get it. I would go out scrapping, and I became very good with working with my hands. Because I was good with my hands, I could have fixed just about anything. People would hire me, and I would make quick money that way.

I was using these newfound gifts for the wrong purpose. I wasn't using them to take care of my family; I was using them for myself so that I could get high. I just slipped further and further. I didn't want for anything. If I wanted that drug, I was capable of making it happen for me. I had connections, so I would borrow. It was becoming so easy because I was adapting to that lifestyle and moving in a way that I never would have before. I was living in this fantasy world, but it was reality; I was taking chances, not realizing that they were endangering my life and my family's life, all the while not caring, sliding deeper and deeper because I'd adapted. I became used to this lifestyle. After so many years, you become used to it. It's your way of living. That's the way I lived; that was natural for me. I didn't feel any kind of way. I became numb to the world and, to be quite frank, I started hating people after all the years of dealing with this issue. There were people, all the church folk, who talked about me when we first got married: "Oh, they are not going to make it." Nothing but negativity.

Nothing but negativity. So my mindset started changing even toward the church, not toward God — that's the one thing: not toward God, but toward the church — because I understood that church folk are just like the people of the world. They gossip, they talk, they spread rumors. But through all of that, the one constant was that I knew my wife was praying. Through all the struggle, through the pressure, through the hard times, through all of that, I was praying too. I was also crying. I was dealing with a part of me that I couldn't get out. There was something in me just ripping, ripping, ripping. No one else could see — at the time, not even my wife — because what was in the physical eye was not the main focus. Still, there was an inner me, the man speaking today, who was trapped in that bubble, crying out. I needed to break out. I had to find my way back home. I had to, and I just kept slipping, falling deeper and deeper into a life of despair, not thinking I would ever get out, succumbing to what my life was. I almost just said, "This is who I am, and this is what I'm going to be." But *the voice.*

So, I remembered that I missed someone important to me. I missed that funeral, and I was in the room getting high. I was in this place where I used to hang out, a very small room. There were sometimes about 12 of us, man, in this small room, and I would smoke crack all day, Other people would just sniff coke, some had reefer, beer, alcohol, liquor. So I was supposed to be at this funeral, and I was in this room getting high. Most people didn't know I was hurting because this person was very close to me. I was hurting, but the reason why I didn't go was because of my appearance. I felt ashamed, and I didn't look that good. I was in it; I was in one of my rough times. I was in bad shape, and I didn't want to go because I thought people — you know, the same church people — would be like, "Oh, did you see Richie? Look how bad he looks." That's what they did back then; they talked about others instead of talking about the person in the coffin. I didn't want to give them the opportunity to shoot me down. So, that's part of the reason why I didn't go to the funeral, along with the fact that I was just getting high.

Most people would say, "Well, why are you just getting high? Why did you do it? Why did you just keep getting high? That's your fault." Yeah, that's my fault. That's my fault, and all of that is good, BUT IF YOU WEREN'T IN MY SHOES, THEN YOU DON'T KNOW WHAT I WAS EXPERIENCING.

"For I know the plans I have for you, declares the LORD, plans to prosper you and not to harm you, plans to give you hope and a future". — *Jeremiah 29:00 NIV*

Jennifer: Watching the man I love disappear, and the impact on our marriage, family and mental health.

The isolation I experienced was so painful, especially knowing that the man I love so deeply was slipping away right before my eyes.

During those days, my husband was and still is a kind, caring man with a big heart. I held on to what I knew my husband to be. *How can this be happening? What would I do? What's going to happen to our family and our marriage?* All these questions were floating around my mind, and no answers were coming fast enough.

As I watched him disappear, this horrible experience continued to seep into every area of our relationship, impacting our family dynamics and crippling my mental health.

I felt as though I was living with a stranger every day. When I looked at him, I saw him, but it was as if he didn't exist.

As this slow yet fast disappearance of my husband fractured the trust, intimacy and dreams of our relationship, I was left with taking on roles and responsibilities in our family. I had no choice and no time to prepare myself to lead our family. I felt that I had no options, and so it was just, *Do your best, Jen.* It brought cycles of disappointment: I would believe that he would change — sometimes, he used to say he would stop, but that didn't happen — only to see him pulled back into addiction more and more. As it continued to escalate, here I was, being the new head of household, trying to keep everything together.

I started to feel resentment and frustration. I was mentally exhausted and couldn't even feel physically exhausted. I was angry for many days but covered it up. At night, I would cry out and ask, *"GOD, PLEASE HELP ME. I DON'T KNOW WHAT I AM DOING HERE. I FEEL AS THOUGH I'M LOSING MY MIND AND NO ONE SEES ME."*

Communication between us continued to deteriorate, and the emotional bond we built together was getting weaker and weaker as the addiction became a powerful third presence in our relationship. It was like having another woman involved in our marriage, and I couldn't get rid of her.

It was like a rerun or repeat; I'd just watch it continue day after day, not feeling that I had the power to say much or do much. Whenever much was said, the conversation would turn into an argument, and I was often scared because I wasn't sure what things would look like on a daily basis. I was careful not to make him angry and keep pressing on because I knew I had to stay strong for our children at all times. Don't get me wrong, Richard is a beautiful man, but that addiction was ugly. When the beautiful man would show up, I was excited yet scared because I never knew when the ugly one would show up. I was always on the lookout.

I lived in shame, guilt, fear and daily stress, and yet I continued to watch. All I could do was pray and stand on the promises of God. The lyrics to "Stand" by Pastor Donnie McClurkin held me close to God; each time I played the song, I drew strength.

(What do you do) when you've done all you can
And it seems like it's never enough
And what do you say when your friends turn away
And you're all alone
Tell me what do you give when you've given your all
And it seems like you can't make it through
Well you just stand, when there's nothing left to do
You just stand, watch the Lord see you through
Yes after you've done all you can, you just stand

Tell me how do you handle the guilt of your past
Tell me how do you deal with the shame
And how can you smile while your heart has been broken
And filled with pain filled with pain
Tell me what do you give when you've given your all
And it seems like you can't make it through
Child you just stand when there's nothing left to do
You just stand watch the Lord see you through
Yes after you've done all you can, you just stand

(Stand) and be sure (and be sure)
Be not entangled in that bondage again, you just stand
(Stand) and endure (and endure)
For God has a purpose yes God has a plan, tell me
(What do you do) When you've done all you can
And it seems like you can't make it through
Child you just...stand (stand) you just stand (stand) stand
(stand)
Don't you dare give up (you just)

Through the storm (stand)

> Stand through the rain (stand)
> Through the hurt (stand)
> Yeah through the pain (you just)
>
> Don't you bow (stand) and don't you bend (stand)
> Don't give up (stand) no don't give in (you just)
> Hold on (stand) , just be strong (stand)
> God will step in (stand), it won't be long no no no(you just)

I consistently took our children to church. I kept myself involved in church to stay occupied and not think about the reality of what lived at home, what was happening at home, what could happen at home, what was going to happen at home, all the what-ifs. I just had to keep watching, keep praying.

There was a time when Rich was coming to church. He was involved in church, and as he got deeper and deeper into the drugs, the hanging out and the weed, it was as if he was fading into the shadows.

He wasn't attending church anymore, and I know that he was hurt by the little things he heard. He felt that no one cared or understood, so attending church at that time didn't matter to him, but I did participate with the kids. It was my lifeline and something that I just knew I had to do. I kept the kids going, kept the kids involved and protected the kids.

I didn't always want the kids to go places. I heard folks thought I was "all that" or "too anti-social," but little did they know it was safer for me to keep my kids close, and I was embarrassed about a lot of things. I was embarrassed to be around people, and I've heard little things myself. I heard whispers, heard people talk, and I just kept to myself and kept pushing. I didn't want to be around people too much. I just wanted to be home, and all I could think was, *What is Rich doing?*

I was concerned about how much he would drink if and when we went out. If he drank too much, it would just lead to one thing after another, and I didn't know what would happen or how things would turn out. Most times, it didn't turn out too good, then here would come the weed and drugs next. He continued to make empty promises, saying he would stop, but he continued again. We had arguments about him leaving to go out. I would say, "Do you have to go hang out?" He would say to me that I was trying to control him, and he has one mother. I wasn't trying to be his mother. I was trying to protect him. I was trying to *save my husband.*

I was trying to keep my husband alive. I didn't know any other way, but we always ended up in an argument. It was always me: me trying to be controlling, me trying to be this or that. While I was living this nightmare, some people would say I was controlling, mean, unfriendly, a baby maker. I heard it all, but they had no idea the hell I was in. They had no idea, but that's what they thought about me. How in the world could I trust anyone and share with them after hearing these different things? I was alone, and all I had was God; I could tell it all to only Him. I did not want Rich to go hang out. I wasn't trying to control him. I just wanted my husband alive, clean from the drugs and the people he was hanging with. I learned what a husband's supposed to be, what a man of God is supposed to be, and I knew Rich wasn't representing that.

I was willing to do anything to get him where he needed to be. I was always asking, "Why do you have to go out tonight? Why do you have to go hang out? Why? Every time they call you, you go running. Why? Why?" Then, more talk: "She wears the pants. She's the boss." SMH. They had no idea. The truth was, I was in a seat that didn't belong to me. I was left to lead the family. Yes, I was the head of the household at the time. The seat did not belong to me; I didn't want it. Sometimes the crying wasn't always just with him or about him. I would sometimes cry thinking about how people were talking about us when they had no clue what we were living with. If people only understood. People real close to me didn't understand. I didn't blame them. I just didn't share it all. I don't blame them at all. And so it hurt to hear rumors, to hear people say things, to see people look in my face and smile after assuming things about me, but I did not have the strength to take them on. I had enough at home to deal with.

Nobody knew how I slept at night — if I did sleep. Nobody knew when I didn't have it; nobody knew why I was borrowing money. Nobody knew about the time when I was homeless; I couldn't eat, but I made sure my kids ate. Our kids were kept intact; they weren't dirty, they went to school every day and they had all that they needed. I had a sister friend who used to hook our kids up. I love and appreciate her for being there during those times in our lives.
While folks were talking, I was drowning, but people didn't know. I marked it well.

While I was hurting, I did something I wouldn't wish on my worst enemy.

But for whatever reason — I don't want to say it had to happen — it happened, and all I had was God. Yes, I had one or two people I could have spoken to, but I didn't tell themt 100% everything. So all I had was God who knew it all, and He was the one I had to lean on totally. I felt I had to have conversations with Him and pray that He would lift me out of this nightmare.

The mental, emotional and verbal abuse was not something that I was used to; I'd never encountered it in all my life, but it happened at that moment in time. I didn't know it was mental abuse at the moment, I didn't know it was emotional abuse at the moment, I didn't know it was verbal abuse at the moment — I didn't even see abuse.

But years later, and as I got fully educated about abuse, I realized it was something I lived through. I don't know if I would rather have been beaten than to have dealt with the mental, emotional and verbal abuse. I used to think maybe it should have been physical abuse. Then, the bruises would hurt, but I'd get over it and heal. Crazy to think this way, but what else was left? I tried to hold our children intact. They were good kids, but they used to argue with each other. Sometimes the girls would get into it; our son got into it with the girls a few times as he got older, and it started making me think, like, *Oh, the residue of all this is coming on my kids. God, please protect my kids. I cannot go through this without You, God.*

I guess this is why some folks were saying we needed therapy. The kids needed it. They didn't get therapy, nor did I — at least not professional therapy — and as much as I was trying to protect my kids, I know this took a toll on them emotionally, and that breaks my heart. For a moment, I felt like a horrible mother because I should have taken care of them better and protected them better. I should have gotten them help because they too were affected. But I did my best; I didn't know what else I could have done at that time. We have one son, and I used to pray that our son wouldn't adopt any of what my husband was experiencing: "We cannot have this addiction latch onto him or our daughters. God, You have to protect my children."

At one point, selfishly or unselfishly, I wasn't even worried about or focused so much on the drug because I knew it was there. Still not knowing how deep it was, I would think he was out there cheating on me. That's what I was thinking, nothing else. Why else would a man be outside all night? Why else would a man not want to be home? That was my only thought. I wasn't heavily concerned about the drug or what it was doing to him, but instead, *This is what's happening, and this is what I'm living with every day.* WHY DID I HAVE TO EXPERIENCE THIS? I didn't talk much about it with people, and I did not share all I was feeling or experiencing. No one knew what was going on inside. I was just hoping for a better husband. If I'm honest, sometimes I pretended I had the greatest home, the greatest marriage.

Emotionally, my heart was a battleground of love, anger, rage, anxiety and sorrow.

It was only God, even after He put people in our path to support us, some of whom ultimately talked about us. It's still God. I still thank Him because it all had a purpose. I'M GOOD. I just refused to feel those types of emotions anymore. I already had enough to deal with, so I didn't even have time for the people who took time to converse about us when they were looking at us from the outside and had no idea what we were living with on the inside.

My husband was the best person in the world to me. Our conversations were great. I used to pretend that if I could only live in the moments when times are great, all would be well. I would wish that when I got home from work, he would be home and just stay home. I would wish for him to date me every day, treat me the way I know I deserve, spend money on me and on us, just lead the family. Don't get me wrong — he wasn't just home, just going out and coming back in. He worked. He was a functioning addict, and I had a front-row seat to watch it just happen. There was a time when he wasn't working; he was just home and still expected me to feed his habit ... and I did. Oh, boy. This part right here is hard to reflect on. I made excuses for why he wasn't working. WHY DID I DO THAT? I blamed the people he hung out with all the time: *IT'S THEIR FAULT.* If they called the house, I wasn't always nice to them when I answered, and I didn't hold back on anything. I know Rich did not like it when I did that, and honestly, it seemed as though he did not care; he demonstrated that by still going out. Here I was, watching the person I married, the person I love, fade away, and

I couldn't do anything about it. But again, my number one focus was, *He's out there with somebody.* Even though I knew that the drug was a thing in his life, it wasn't a heavy focus. Honestly, I was just thinking about if he was with another woman and what would that do to our marriage, not thinking or realizing that the addiction was ripping up our marriage day after day. Sometimes I would talk out loud to myself and say, GET YOUR HEAD ON RIGHT, JEN. STOP THINKING ABOUT SOME OTHER WOMAN AND SEE WHAT'S REALLY HAPPENING. Eventually, I had to get my thoughts right, but I'll be honest — how could I when my world was falling apart? But that didn't stop me from praying. I was praying; I was fasting. The kids were praying. I was putting oil in his shoes, laying my hands on his clothes and going into the closet. Our middle child was right there with me, doing the same, praying standing up, praying laying down. Praying and crying was my best at the time, just hoping for relief, hoping for a breakthrough because I felt like I couldn't do it.

I tried. I cooked, I cleaned, I was with him intimately even when I didn't want to be. I just tried to do what I thought a wife should've done and be what a wife should've been. I thought maybe that would help, that would make him be home, that would make him stop. I DID ALL THOSE THINGS AND NOTHING HAPPENED FAST ENOUGH. If he asked for $5, I would give it to him freely. Whatever he asked, I gave it, and sometimes I wasn't just giving it — I was *forgiving* it. I was also giving it out of fear; I didn't want to cause an argument because he was probably going to take it anyway, so I just did it. I just had to watch and watch him take and take, but the nights when he wasn't home or while the kids were asleep, I spent those times crying and crying. I cried until no tears were coming out. I used to hear that saying and didn't know it existed until I experienced it myself. I cried until I could touch my face and no tears were falling. Not knowing what else to do, what else was left to do, I just continued to occupy the front row seat and watch the man I love, the man I know to be wonderful, the man I know to have a beautiful heart destroy himself and us.

I knew God had a calling on his life, and I believed that God had put him in my life for a reason; I told myself it was just a process. I'm sorry — *process my behind*. I wanted it over already. The simultaneous inconsistency and consistency in the things that were breaking the family and our marriage was a bit much to manage. WHEN WOULD CHANGE COME? WHEN WOULD RESCUE COME? WHEN WOULD THIS END? I held it all in and kept pushing once again. I operated as a wife, a father and a mother, everything that our children needed. Some days, he would say, "Jen, I'm going to stop today," or whatever day he would say, but it would not happen — or it would happen for a few days only for him to go right back to it, deeper and deeper each time. In the beginning, when I would hear him say he was going to stop, I would get excited — *Yes, it's happening!* — and then nothing. Inwardly, I was tired and ashamed and didn't want anyone to know what I was feeling. If I'm honest, there were moments when I thought about just taking my life: *Maybe he'll be better because now, he has to be here for the kids.* I did not know all of the emotions I was experiencing at the time, but I clearly remember the late nights, the lonely nights, the worrisome nights, the scary nights spent wondering what was going to happen.

At that time, mental health wasn't a term that I used, or I probably wasn't used to hearing it. But looking back, I can say that my mental health was deteriorating, probably faster than I thought. I was walking around strongly. I went to work every day. I took care of the home and our kids. Shamefully, I begged people for money. Sometimes I couldn't pay it back. Oh, God, why? There were times when the rent couldn't be paid, and we almost ended up on the street. This was before Rich became a super and we did not have to pay rent; even then, there were bills to be paid and a home to take care of, and I still found myself asking people for help. I had a good friend whom I asked for help more than once, and she graciously helped me financially. I had people who saw me dressed well and clean. Our kids were dressed well and smelled good. They didn't look horrible. You couldn't tell that there was a dysfunction in our home at all; our kids went to school every day.

I never really talked about it with my kids. I didn't know what they were feeling or knew. All I cared about was protecting them and making sure they were good. Our middle daughter was always right at my hem, so she knew, but people thought we were good. Like I said, I pretended that my world wasn't falling apart. I pretended that I had a husband when I didn't.

He was always around for our kids, but I did not think he was the father they needed during those years. There were times when he would pick them up from school and play with them; those were moments I cherished because at any given time, he could leave to continue his addiction. Yet, I still had to lead our family so that we wouldn't collapse. I even thought that maybe I should go on drugs too.

I don't know what I was thinking, but I did think that. *What would that look like?* But I only thought that for, like, three seconds because I was on the outside, looking in at him. It wasn't something I wanted to experience, but I was just trying to think of anything I could do while I watched the man I love keep going through the revolving doors of his addiction. I was determined to be the wife God called me to be. I was determined to be there. I was determined to not let go. I was determined to stay strong. In the beginning, there was a thought of, *I'm going to prove people wrong.* After that, though, I was just determined not to give up. But while being determined, I was tired. I was mentally, emotionally and physically tired, but somehow, I kept my strength. I developed a spirit of resilience like none other, and I kept going, not knowing when it was going to break or what the break would look like. I would hear people say, "You know he's going to hit rock bottom."

What does that mean? I felt like he hit it a few times and nothing happened. So what does that mean? After a while, I didn't even want to hear that phrase. Like, what does "rock bottom" mean for real? I wished people would just shut up and stop talking as if they knew. When I first heard it, I was like, *Good. When rock bottom comes, oh! That means it's going to be over, and we're going to be great.* But rock bottom came so many times, I was like, *It ain't happening.* It didn't happen. Like, what would it take? WHAT WOULD IT TAKE?

And I remember one night while praying, God was just so clear for me to take my hands off. I didn't listen; I didn't understand at first. But as I was going through this, and as time went by, I realized: "Take your hands off" *means* "Take your hands OFF."

I told myself, *Stop trying to control this within yourself, and let God be in control. Whatever happens happens; just trust God.* In the beginning, I tried to listen to God, but it was hard. It was hard to keep watching Rich be this way. There were times when he would come home, or times when he was already home and having his beer, and he would smoke — yup, he smoked *in the house* and tried to hide it so the children would not know. Of course there were arguments about that. Two of our children were asthmatic! What the h-e-double-hockey-sticks was wrong with him? What the what? What was he thinking? There were times when he would throw up and I was right there, saying to myself, *I've got to help him; he's my husband. I'm called to be his helpmate no matter what. Called to be his wife. For better or worse — forget the "richer or poorer" part.*

There were moments when I would have conversations with myself: *Your mother did not raise you to be this stupid. Your mother didn't raise you to be this way. What kind of mother are you? What are you showing your daughters? They have to be here to watch this, to watch him talk to you the way he talks to you sometimes, to watch him take from you, to watch you work this hard to keep the family afloat. WHAT ARE YOU DOING, JEN?* I asked myself all these questions, and I didn't know the answers to any of them.

I was so confused, but I knew I somehow had to trust God. But who was I fooling? At the time, my trust was partial, and that doesn't work with God. Either you're in or you're out. I'm a wife first, and I have to be there for my husband. That doesn't mean, — and it didn't mean at the time — that I had to not care for my kids, but I could do both. I thought I was doing both at the time, and I thought I was doing the best that I could while watching my husband deteriorate. Other times, I believed that he was lazy and only cared about himself. Ultimately, it was mental and emotional abuse. I used to hear those words and be like, "No, no, my husband's not abusive," but both mental abuse and emotional abuse were present. (WOW. I SAID IT OUT LOUD AND HEARD MYSELF!) I used to go in the bathroom, open up the medicine cabinet and take a look at the pills. I'd just stand there and think about the ways I could end it all: *I can end it now because I'm trying everything, everything for him to stop, and nothing's working.* Clearly, I was back to thinking I could solve this and not thinking at all about what God said. Meanwhile, Rich kept going out, staying out longer and later. *Nothing's working. What am I going to do?* And I kept watching. I'M TIRED!!

Every time I walked out of our house, I had to put on a mask. I couldn't tell it all to anyone. I used to talk to one or two people but didn't tell them everything. I tried to make it nice so that no one would think horrible things of him, but I never really shared the rawness of what I felt, the things I felt like doing to myself or the things I felt like doing to him — Shoot, *he's behaving as if his life means nothing. Maybe he should end his, then.* I know that I sound horrible. I have no idea what hell is like, and if it's anything like what I experienced, then I want no parts of it.

I used to pray so much that at one point, I stopped praying, and all I was saying was just "Jesus." Just Jesus. It used to be praying hard and naming things. It used to be, "Jesus, get me out of this. Jesus, take me out of this. Jesus, make it stop. Jesus, make the pain stop. Jesus, please, please help him. Please save him. Jesus, wherever he's at right now, please break the taste out of his mouth. God, just do something, anything, please." I was so tired. I didn't know what else to do. I'd done everything, even things I shouldn't have, like lie about who I am. I wasn't true to myself, and I wasn't true about who or what I was experiencing to other people who loved and cared about me. Then, there were the people who were just nosey and wanted to be in our business. And then, there were the other people who just believed what they saw, but that was because I *let* them see that. I didn't complain; I kept living. One time, I asked Rich's sister to meet me to talk and share. I could see in her face that some of it was hard to hear, not just because it was her brother but because she was hearing me share, as a person, what was happening to me and our family. It was my first time sharing this much, yet I still did not share it all. I just had to tell somebody.

While I was going through the pain and the hurt that I felt at that time in my marriage, people who thought we were good. But I'm not mad at them, at least not now, because I realize that's the picture I painted. I painted a picture that I was good, that my family was good. Certain people would see me ask for money or ask for things, and they didn't believe that I needed it because they didn't know my true circumstances. I did not have it all the time, and yes, sometimes I played it off or lied as if I had it all together just to keep people out of my business. I took one day at a time and just tried to make it work.

For our 10th anniversary, I told Richard that I wanted us to renew our wedding vows. When we first got married, we got married in shorts in our pastor's/aunt's office, and it was cute and beautiful. I always wanted a wedding, and our 10th anniversary seemed to be the best time to do it. I am slightly embarrassed to say that I felt like if we did this, it would help, and it would renew his mindset and maybe rid him of the drugs...? I know that sounds crazy and dumb, but I was willing to try anything to save him and our relationship. I loved him. We didn't even really have the money to do this 100%, but God made a way through family and friends. I was so ashamed yet grateful. It was a beautiful ceremony, and for a very, very short moment, I had my husband — but just after that very, very short moment, things seemed to get worse.

Going back to one difficult time that I can remember: My mom was sick, and I had to take care of my her. I was going back and forth to do so, and at one point, she ended up in the hospital. Mom was in the hospital for a while, and I continued to visit her. This particular day, I wanted to go back to see my mom, but Rich didn't want me to go because he wanted things his way. He wanted to leave and go smoke and God knows whatever, but I wanted to get to my mom. I knew my mom was dying, and I wanted to go back and see her. It was just unseemly and heartless that he didn't want me to go, and he had me up against the wall — just had me there; he didn't want me to go. Well, that day, I lost my mom, and I didn't get to see her before she passed. I was devastated and angry all at the same time. I hated him for a long time for not letting leave when I wanted to. I never did that to his mother. I was there for him and his mom all the time; even on the days when he wasn't in the house, I was there with his mom. But I couldn't get the same thing back for my mom, and I had a missed opportunity because of him. That's how I felt. That thing hurt like none other, and I hated him for it.

I feel like that's when things started turning in my head, and

I began to gain some strength. I started to get better in how I handled all of this. I prayed and prayed. I had many songs that I liked to listen to, various worship songs that stuck with me and helped me carry through during this time. Another one was "Encourage Yourself" by Donald Lawrence; I used to play that over and over too. I needed to encourage myself, especially during my low times. I wasn't telling people much, so I only had myself to lean on for encouragement, and I kept some of the song lyrics on repeat in my mind and heart. You know, sometimes you have to speak a word over yourself. Depression is all around, but God is a present help. Well, the enemy created walls, but remember: Giants do fall. Speak a word over yourself. Encourage yourself. Encourage yourself. I knew I had to speak victory over myself during that time. Most may have thought it was a test, but it felt like torture.

I leaned on Philippians, 4:13; I leaned on Hebrews, 11:1. I had to have faith. But Proverbs 3, 5 and 6 stuck with me. In particular, Hebrews 11 and Proverbs 3, 5 and 6 stuck with me because I had to trust. I had to take my hands off. I had to stop trying to control or be in control or control this because this was way bigger than me. I had to stop leaning on my own understanding. This is not about me and never was, but it was hard because I was watching the man whom I love — and, in the same breath, the man with whom I felt angry all the time — just fade away right in front of me. During these times, I had to develop. I had low self-esteem. I knew I had depression, and I knew I had built-up anger, but I covered it all up when I left the house so no one could see. When we reached a space in our life, in our relationship or in our marriage where we went through a phase of homelessness, broke up or, as some might say, separated from each other, my good friends were shocked when they learned about it. I understood. I couldn't say, "Why are you shocked?"

They were shocked because they saw me at work every day with a smile on my face, all while being in the classroom with kids. I was helping other women and parents at my job who were going through abuse. I was the one they were leaning on, helping them while I was drowning, while I was dying on the inside. I didn't tell them; I was just there for them because it gave me strength to carry on.. So when my colleagues found out and were shocked, I understood. They couldn't believe that I went on for that long and that no one knew, but that's what I did. I masked it the best way I could. It was hard, but I did it. I had to do that for my kids, to protect them — at least I thought that was important to me. I was trying to save my husband, but everything I tried didn't work. I just kept watching this man fade away. I felt alone. Many times, I felt like I couldn't tell anyone the truth. What would they say? When the truth was told to some, I would hear things like, "You should have left him," and "Why did you stand with him?"

I didn't want to hear that. I strongly believed that God put us together and we would get through this. But it was the hardest thing I had to experience. My mom and my dad — God bless them, they're no longer here — didn't know. My mom wasn't here for all of it, and my dad didn't know. My sisters didn't know what I went through. No one knew, and whatever little bit people heard, they didn't hear it all. No one knew.

I couldn't tell anyone that I wanted to die. I couldn't tell anyone that I wanted to hurt him. I was so tired. All I wanted to do was protect the kids and help him, but he didn't want it.

I wanted him to stop, and I was like, "God, can you just make it stop? Can you make it go away? Enough is enough." He loved drugs more than he loved me. He loved his friends and hanging out with them more than he did me. Getting him to hang with me was like pulling teeth, but he had no problem going to hang with the guys to smoke.

What's wrong with me? Why would he do this to me? Why won't he stop? Doesn't he see me hurting? What the hell is wrong with him? He would see me cry and say I was doing too much, being whiny and talking too much, not understanding what I was really feeling on the inside.

Am I not his wife? Like, why? None of it made sense, and I must have lost a huge part of my mind. I asked myself all these questions. *I did everything that I thought I was supposed to do as a wife. My mom raised a good girl.* These are all the things I was saying. *He has a good woman. I'm not looking for anybody else, so why can't all this just go away?*

I just want my marriage. I just want my husband. Like, why? Why can't he just quit? Why? Those are the questions I asked: Why? "About three in the afternoon, Jesus cried out in a loud voice, 'Eli, Eli, lema sabachthani?'" (Translation:"My God, my God, why have You forsaken me?") — *Matthew 27:46 NIV*

CHAPTER 3

HITTING ROCK BOTTOM

Richard: The lowest point — losing control and realizing the extent of the damage

When I was younger, I liked to look and dress good. We used to call it "getting fresh," and I stood fresh. I now see how crack took control of my life. I could see differences in my appearance. I wouldn't cut my hair and my hand-me-down clothes were often dirty. I wasn't buying clothes because all my money was going to get high.

Thank God I had hot water and a place to shower because if I didn't, I probably wouldn't have showered. My fingertips were all chewed up from popping the lighter and holding the crack pipe; it was literally eating my skin away. I would hide my hands because I didn't want people to notice. My skin wasn't clear; my mind wasn't clear. I was just running the streets, looking and feeling tired — but the crack. That was all I was living for, and that's when I knew I was in the danger zone. But again, I just couldn't stop.

I just wanted more. I wanted to keep going more, you know. I didn't feel like I needed sleep. I didn't feel like I needed family.

I didn't feel like I needed anybody. All I wanted was to smoke the pipe.

The pipe was my life. All the while, there was always a voice telling me, *You shouldn't be living this way.* But I would ignore it, and I would go back to what I knew.

You know, guys, this book is a journey, and it's hard for me to speak about some things, but I have to be open. I want this to resonate with whoever may be reading this. There was always hope. And that voice that I spoke about — it wasn't my wife, it wasn't my children, it wasn't a family member or a friend. It was always a gentle voice that would say, *I'm here. I see you. I'm waiting for you, and I care for you.*

I grew accustomed to this world of darkness. It was my life, and I did not see a way out of it. That's who I was, but the voice I was ignoring kept telling me, *This is not who you are.*

It brings me to the scripture Ephesians 6:12, — we wrestle not against flesh and blood but against principalities, the powers of the air. I understand now. This thing that had a hold of me was a demon. That's what I recognize crack cocaine or any drug as. It's a demon put there to destroy you, to take you out of who you are.

People think that rock bottom is when something happens, and it makes you stop. Rock bottom is when you do things that you would never see yourself doing. Rock bottom is not just one thing — rock bottom is several things.

Looking back, I know now that I couldn't beat this thing by myself. I hit rock bottom, selling, stealing and taking money out of my wife's purse, which she never knew. I was seeing myself and saying, *Don't do it. Don't do it.* But I was at rock bottom, finally coming to the realization that I had to listen to the voice. It was God calling me to stop.

So I gave myself to Christ. I gave it over to Him. *"Out of the depths [of distress] I have cried to You, O Lord." — Psalm 130:1 AMP*

Jennifer: The pain of seeing him hit rock bottom and the fear of losing him forever

I knew he used to steal from me and maybe the kids. I knew. I used to hide as much as I could, but he took and took from me. In the beginning — I just didn't know it then — there was denial. I still didn't know 100% what type of drug, what it did or the effects it had, and if I'm being honest, I did not even research it back then. All I knew was that it was a drug, and it was bad. Man, I sound ignorant.

My mind goes back to the many nights seeing him when he came through the doors — not even nights, *mornings*. I would see him stumble and hear the slurred speech; he would want to make love, and I would try not to upset him by saying no. There were even times when he came home and ended up sleeping on the floor or crashed out on the couch.

After a while, he was unrecognizable. He wasn't the person I fell in love with, and yet, I clung to memories of the man he was and hoped for a glimpse of the person I fell in love with to show up.

He was not the Rich I met in the beginning. Even though he was smoking and on drugs then, things just got progressively worse, and I had no idea when rock bottom was going to show up. Then, reality sat in, and I now know what I was dealing with.

The love I have for Richard compelled me to support him, hoping he would live and not die, and so there was always a constant thought of losing him. I'm not just talking about getting up and leaving him — I feared losing him to death. I feared that I would get a call one night, or something was going to happen because he was doing drugs. The pain of seeing my husband, the man I married, drowning while I stood by helpless, and not knowing what I could truly do, was soul-crushing.

I watched the man I love slowly spiral into darkness, and I felt as though there was nothing I could say or do to reach him. I would go to sleep hoping that tomorrow would be better, and I would wake up thinking, *This is the day*, hoping that the throbbing in my heart would go away. The fear of losing him forever grew within me. I didn't physically display it, but it was a relentless presence, like a dark shadow that would not go away, a thunderstorm with an uncertain end.

One or two days after having an amazing worship time with God in a church that I visited, I bared myself to Him once again. I gave Him everything that I had, everything within me, even everything I had financially. I just gave it all to God.

Then, the explosion happened where I thought we'd hit rock bottom. We were in the kitchen, and Rich was just being a nag; we were going back and forth. I didn't feel like being bothered at that point. I was just tired, and I didn't want to hear his voice anymore. I was at my end; I just couldn't do it anymore. I literally felt something different within me. I didn't want to argue, I didn't want to fight, I didn't want to talk to him, I just didn't want to be bothered. So he just kept being a nag. If my memory serves me right, I think he wanted to be intimate or something, but I had no interest. I had no idea at this point, but he was just a nag.

Then, he got upset, and I got hit on the ear. I really can't remember how the hit came about, but I know I got hit on the ear. I felt it, and I just cried and cried. I became scared because now, this was starting to look and feel different. *He hit me just because he wanted to. What? Why?* Although it wasn't a direct hit, it felt like it, and all I could feel at the time was fear, not knowing what was next.

Our middle child was in that same area where it all happened. She saw her mom being this way, being emotional. I can remember that at that point, I left home. I got in my car and drove a little bit, but I came back — and when I came back, the cops were there, and I had to identify that it was Rich. All I was thinking was, *He hit me with kids in the house*, and so I pointed him out and they arrested him. The next thing I remember is that I was on my way to the hospital, so I must have blacked out or collapsed or something, but I was on my way to the hospital. I was at the hospital for a little while, and then I got discharged and came home.

We packed up and left, the children and I. We packed up as much as we could, which wasn't much, and we left everything else behind — everything we'd worked for, everything we'd purchased for our kids. Our kids had Barbie dolls and Barbie dollhouses; they had everything they wanted, and we left it all behind. Our son had his different games and different things. We just left everything., I had personal papers, all left behind. We just took what we could at the time because in my mind, he was coming back, and we just had to go. I'd hit my rock bottom.

I'm not sure if it was his rock bottom, but it was mine, and there's nothing more I could have done to fix him. I just was at my wit's end. *There's nothing left for me to do.* But what was ironic to me is that just a couple of days after having an encounter with God, after giving God everything I had, down to the last dollar that I had — literally — this happened. All I could've said to God during that moment was, "God it's all in Your hands. Do whatever." Who would have thought this would happen after the time I had with God? I did not know what was going to happen next. Who would have thought this would be my rock bottom or that this is what my rock bottom would look like? I had to process, and quickly, because the hit, the cops, the craziness my children were exposed to — and then homelessness. WE WERE HOMELESS! Oh, my God. That happened. We didn't have a home anymore. So I asked myself, *What are we going to do?*

I could only hope that this wasn't the end of us and that it was the beginning of something great, but truth be told, I was more scared than ever. I had no idea what was next, but something broke in me.

"The Lord is near to the heartbroken and He saves those who are crushed in spirit [contirte in heart, truly sorry for their sin]." — Psalms 34:18 AMP

CHAPTER 4

A Moment of Clarity

Richard: What led me to seek help — confrontation with my own reality

As a kid, I had anger issues. A lot of it stemmed from jealousy, sometimes feeling as if I was an outcast from my immediate family. Why did I feel that way? I don't know, but I do know that I was feeling that way. My anger sometimes arose in our marriage. There was this one time when Jen and I were arguing about Jenny always going to visit her mother in the hospital. Jen's mom had been sick for some time. This one particular day, she was leaving to go see her, and I didn't want her to go because I wanted to go out myself. As she was leaving, I said to her, "I wish your mother would die already." As those words left my mouth, I said to myself, *What did you just say?* Needless to say, her mother passed away that day. *Damn.* I hated myself. So what did I do? Yeah — I went out and got high.

Well, I can't take what I had said back, so what use would it be for me to say sorry? I'm going to move like nothing happened. That was my thought process. The person I am today would have never said those words. I still live with that guilt to this very day. I have asked forgiveness from both her and God since then.

That was just one of many hard days and battles yet to come. We started struggling financially. We would fall behind in rent, and Jen would have to borrow money from people. I no longer was the head of the household. I was just there freeloading, and when I did make money or work, all the money went to drugs. So I got a job at a Head Start program just around the corner from where we lived. On payday, I would get my check and not come home until the next morning, hoping that Jen would have left for work already. I knew if she was home, there was going to be an argument, and I didn't want to hear it. Looking back now, I don't know why she didn't leave me.

At this point, I was starting to think God wasn't listening. So one day, I set my family down and told them we were going to become Muslims. You might ask, "But Richard, how would that have helped you?" But my thinking was that Islam was more disciplined. To be honest, the church folk were phony to me — not all of them, but nonetheless, the phoniness was there. Let me tell you, when God has a plan, it works for your good.

A few months after saying we were going to be Muslims, God started working. Jen was on a women's retreat somewhere in the mountains, and I was at home. I'd just finished getting high and was lying on my couch when I heard the voice of the Lord say, "YOU MUST CONFESS YOUR SINS." My first reaction was to call Jen, so I called her right away. I told her I had to tell her something, and she told me she wanted to tell me something. So I told her to tell me what she had to tell me first, and she said God told her that I had to confess my sins. I'm not sure if it was that Sunday or the Sunday after Jenny had come from the retreat. All I knew was that I couldn't wait to get to church that Sunday; I was like, *Okay, I'm going to confess my sins.* On Sundays in my church, there's usually a handful of people, but on this particular Sunday, the church was packed to the point of overflow.

When I walked in those doors, I was so nervous. I was like, *I don't know any of these people.* I saw all these strange faces, and I didn't want to confess. I was scared. It just so happened that a young man was sitting in the seat I normally would have taken, so I had to sit in the back of the church. He got up and confessed his sins — it was my confession, the same exact testimony, right then and there. I knew I had to confess my sins, and I stood up right after him. In front of the whole church, I confessed that I was addicted to crack and that I was smoking crack. I knew that most of my family members already knew, but I felt like a burden was lifted just from me openly saying it. But that's not where the story ends. It was about a year after my testimony, and I was still getting high. Here's where the breaking started to happen.

Jen and I worked for the same Head Start program. We were on spring break, and the Head Start program was closed down. As the janitor, my responsibility was to go in and prepare the building for staff and students upon their return. So I came home that day, and Jenny was by the stove. I believe I was asking her to be intimate with me. She was ignoring me, and I got mad. I felt like I was being disrespected, and it bothered me. I didn't mean to do it, but I raised my elbow hard and quickly, and because I was standing so close to her, it popped her in the ear. I was like, "You hear me now?" She was shocked, you know, because I'd never put my hands on her. We'd had arguments, but I'd never put my hands on her. She was crying, and then she left the house, I guess. That's when things got kind of crazy. The cops were called on me. They came, I got arrested and I spent the night in jail. I came home the next day, and my house looked like a tornado hit it because Jen and the kids were moving fast to get out before I came home. Coming home to see my house in a wreck hit me hard, man. I had to sit there alone — *Wow, my family is not here. What is going on?* So that night, I was running through all kinds of emotions. I was angry.

I was angry at her; I was angry at people. I was blaming the world. Then, I became sad. I started crying and blaming myself, and that's when it started to sink in that my family left. *Well, this is it. There's nothing else here for me.* So I decided I didn't want to live anymore. Since I don't like pain, I knew I wasn't going to cut my wrists or jump out the window. I tried to think of the quickest and easiest way out, and I found a full bottle of pills on the dresser. *That should work, I figured. I'll just lie down and go to sleep, and maybe I won't wake up.*

The next day, I woke up, and the sun was beaming bright on me. God just woke me up. The Holy Spirit was right there in the room with me. Something just took over me, and I threw my hands up. I was like, "All right, God. I surrender," and from that moment, my journey, my walk and my life would never be the same again.

"For I consider [from the standpoint of faith] that the sufferings of the present life are not worthy to be compared with the glory that is about to be revealed to us and in us!" — Romans 8:18 AMP

Jennifer: The moment I realized that I couldn't "fix" him and had to support him in finding help.

The love I have for Richard compelled me to support him, hoping he would overcome his struggles. But hurt and sadness always arises from the broken promises and lies of ("I'll stop") neglect and loneliness during this tumultuous time of our lives. For years, I tried to fix Rich while shouldering the responsibilities alone and feeling exhausted. I did all types of things to help or make things better. I used to think that I could have helped or done something to make it better: *Maybe it's my fault. Maybe I'm not being the wife I should be.*

I was living with the uncertainty, not knowing, praying and waiting for things to get better. I played awful mental games on myself, saying that maybe I needed to lose weight and be slimmer. I thought about all these things. I tried to fix him by talking to him, giving him what he asked for each time, trying not to argue, trying to act as if I was happy when I was certainly wasn't. I was just doing things that I thought would help and that I thought would fix him, but I failed each time. I tried everything. I said yes to making love even when I didn't want to. I pretended a lot of times. I cooked; I cleaned. The only thing I did not do was DRUGS! *WHAT THE HECK IS LEFT FOR ME TO DO TO MAKE THIS MAN STOP?*

I was trying to make him better. I was trying to make him stop. I did it for a long time. He used to come home without money after getting paid and had the nerve to ask me for money ... and I gave it to him. WHAT IN THE WORLD WAS WRONG WITH ME? *Why am I doing this?* I would borrow money from people to take care of my home, and then he would sneak and take it. If I resisted, then there would be an argument, so I would give in just because I didn't want to fight. I just wanted him to stop. But then, as time went on, I kept asking myself these questions: *WHAT ARE YOU DOING? You're out here pretending to be a happy wife in a happy home as if he's not doing anything wrong. He's not loving you like you want to be loved. He's not holding you like you want to be held.* There were nights and days when I just wanted to be held. I wanted to hear, "I love you," and "You look beautiful." I loved to dress and look good to hear somebody tell me I looked good. I didn't have my husband telling me that. Instead, I had my husband coming home and taking money from me, or pawning this or doing that, but not loving me like I wanted to be loved. And so, after some time, I was just like, *I can't keep going on like this. You can't fix him, Jen. What are you going to do?*

Eventually, clarity set in, and I can see now. I had made plans to attend a women's retreat, just to get clarity and answers. While I was planning, Rich was still getting high, frustrated and angry at God. At one point, he talked about us being Muslims. That for sure wasn't happening. However, I was still focused on God, still leaning on Him, still hoping that there was something at the end of this rainbow. It's ironic that I use the word rainbow because the rainbow is known to be beautiful, but everything that was going on seemed to be so ugly.

But in the midst of it all, there was still beauty. There was still love — God's love — and so I leaned on God. I fussed, I cried, I did everything I could think of with God. I attended the women's retreat with the church, and at this point, some of the women were partially aware of what I'd been experiencing.

The retreat was on a mountain somewhere in Pennsylvania, and I went with an expectation to hear from God. He needed to do something. I can't even count how many times I felt like I was in the face of God, begging and pleading for something to break. Meanwhile, I knew that God had already spoken to me and said what I needed to do — but I doubted His plan, and honestly, I did not think it was going to happen fast enough. I just wanted it to happen without me removing my hands. However, God met me at that retreat, and we had a prayer. I bared myself before God once again, but it felt different this time. I clearly heard God tell me that Rich needed to confess his sins. He needed to open his mouth, truly confess and give it all to God. I burst into tears, and the other women were consoling me as the tears flowed down my cheeks. I had my moment with God on the mountaintop. After my time with God, Rich called me, and I was eager to talk to him. He sounded eager to talk to me too. He said, "I got something to tell you," and I said, "I got something to tell you."

He told me to go first, and I said, "Rich, you've got to confess your sins."

He then shared how he heard God's voice telling him the same thing. I broke down in tears; I couldn't believe that the same God who was on the mountaintop with me was in our living room in Brooklyn talking to Rich. Honestly, I wasn't sure by then if he was high or sober, but God was talking to him — another sign for me to know that God was in the midst and He was hearing me. I could now just let Him go ahead and do what He had to do.

I was still going after God, still talking to God, still pleading with God because things could still happen, even after that. I still felt like I needed to stay in the face of God. I had moments when I was wondering if I should leave, but I didn't feel like God was telling me to leave Rich.

I'd already been praying and putting oil in his clothes, like I said before — you know, oil in his shoes, oil on the door. I was insane with the oil, just oiling up everywhere and everything. One night, my pastor and I went to a church service, and I was like, "God, you got to do something. What's the delay, Lord? It was a good Word I heard that night, but when it came time to give, I had nothing left in me. I was tired, and at the end, I gave myself and EVERYTHING TO GOD. I had to surrender to God. I only had $150 on me; it was all the cash I had. I was crying and I was just so tired, and so I said, "God, this is all I got." I put the money in the offering basket and walked away. The bishop called me back said to me, "That was your last that you put in there. God is going to meet your needs."

I wept, and I wept, and I wept. I didn't say anything out loud to anybody. The conversations that I was having in my head at the church were between me and God, with me telling God I would surrender. I didn't talk out loud, and after hearing it come out of the Bishop's mouth, I said to myself, *God, this is it.* I didn't even know what life was going to look like. I didn't know what was going to happen. All I knew was that I couldn't do it anymore. *I can't fix him; I don't have anything left. I'm sick and tired of being tired.* I even felt like I didn't want the marriage anymore. I just had nothing left.

I couldn't do it. Who would want to keep being spoken to any kind of way? I was tired of being abused, tired of not feeling loved, tired of being there for everyone, tired of being in a role that didn't belong to me (HEAD OF THE HOUSE), tired of faking it till I couldn't make it, just tired — and I couldn't fix him. So I had to give everything over to God and say, "God, here. Have your way," knowing that my way wasn't working. What was different this time? I prayed and did all this stuff before. What was different? I know for sure I felt empty. I had nothing left to give. I wanted out.

"Trust in and rely confidently on the Lord with all your heart, and do not rely on your own insight or understanding." — Proverbs 3:5 AMP

CHAPTER 5

SEEKING HELP TOGETHER

Richard: My journey to rehab, the initial resistance and learning to accept I needed help

There I was, all by my lonesome self, and some days had passed. I remember the first day I tried to call Jenny. She wouldn't pick up the phone. She didn't want to talk to me, and I felt like no one was around. So my old nature started kicking in, and I went back to getting high. I was just going through the motions because that's what I was used to doing, but it was different this time around. I didn't enjoy getting high like I used to; I was just doing it because I wanted to have people around me. I went back to my old hangout, where all my old friends were. They were like my family. I felt like my whole family had turned their backs on me.

That's when I started thinking that no one cared for me, but God always has a ram in the bush, so my younger brother opened his home to me. While staying there, I called different rehab programs. I found this one place in Queens and waited there for hours only for them to tell me they couldn't take me in because I didn't have any drugs in my system. I didn't have the money to get back home, and I was stuck out there, man. I called and asked a family member for a favor, and they made me wait for so long, which it hurt me. Then, when they picked me up, they made me feel so low with how they talked and treated me; we got into a heated argument. While I was in the car, we got to a certain point by the J train, and I was like, "Yo, you know what? Just let me out here." Before getting out, I had a few choice words for him. Then, I got out of the car and made my way back to Brooklyn. The reason why I was going back there was because I had some loose ends to tie up.

Eventually, my siblings wanted to have an intervention with me. They encouraged me to go seek help. While they were talking to me, I was saying to myself, *I already tried to get into rehab; I couldn't get in. God already delivered me. He already set me free; he healed me.* For whom the son sets free is free indeed. I knew I didn't really need to go anywhere; I was just going to do this to prove to people what I knew God had already proven to me. So I went to detox just for people's sake, and I spent five days there. That's the only kind of rehab I did. I am not encouraging anyone to not go into rehab — that is ultimately a personal choice — but I would like to encourage you to rely on the source that is God.

He is the one who truly completes the work. You must repent and turn your sinful life around, not to please people, for prestige or for a title but because you want God in your life. If you want to be free from something, and I mean if you want to *really* be set free, then that's when you'll be delivered from stuff. You have to see yourself wanting it and picture yourself already there.

The scanned letters in this chapter represents, when Richard was going through his healing process while he and Jennifer were separated. Journaling and expressing his deep feelings to Jennifer in his writings.

> Please Jenny I'am begging you
> See me one more time. I wish
> you would just hear me it was
> the drugs jenny. My heart is
> smash please don't leave me please.
> I am so sorry. When I go to
> the hospital will you come and
> see me please. So we can talk
> I will do right can My tears
> are all dry

I have to digress. Even before all of this, I told you I was trying to call Jenny on the phone, and she would never pick up.

I remember the first time I got to hear her voice on the phone. I called, and she said she would talk to me, and I got to hear her voice. It was just like that beaming light I saw the day when God was in the room with me and I surrendered to Him. My heart just opened up, and I knew when we got off the phone that we were going to be all right. I would get to talk to Jenny at times, and then I got to talk to the kids, and then God started making ways for Jenny and I to see each other. I remember we saw each other for my birthday. We had a nice time, but it went by quickly because she had to go back to work. I didn't want her to leave. I remember riding the train back to Long Island and saying "God, this is hard," but I had to walk through it, and God was with me.

April 26, 2013

By now I thought my pain would've been gone. But it's still sometime hurts to see my family going through this. Got keep the faith, my wife reminded me today how I turn my back on God. What was I thinking, that man always done for me. Even till this very day he's looking out for me. Sorry lord I am free now keep me on the right track.

There is no looking back must stay focus. If anyone tells you that you can't do it, believe me you can. It took me losing my family to see God, and how much they meant to me. Miss having them around. Last friday they came out to long island and stay the night and part of the day on Saturday. That was nice, the feeling I felt I can't explain. After God they mean the most to me. I hope one day soon this ordeal will end. Want to sleep next to my wife again. She is so pretty both on the inside and out.

My life is coming back together again. Can't wait to go to court. Finicall she is struggling as well as me. But God told me last week we will be ok. Praying I get a new job cause my old one just anit gettin it.

She told me today she misses me. I miss her just as much, boy this is hard.

I think a couple of days later, around the weekend, Jen was like, "All right, I'm going to come out and bring the kids, and we're just going to hang out." We hung out for the whole weekend at my brother's house, and then they had to leave to go back to either Jen's father's house or a friend's house where they were staying. The kids had to go to school, and she had to go to work on Monday.

> April, 28, 2010
>
> Just came to the realization the only people that matter, is my wife & kids. If they forgive me and God forgives me no one else matter. But it must be known if God forgives you than I must forgive you also. 2 Corinthians 2d
>
> People say they love you but in their heart is something different. I love everyone maybe I don't like their ways, but I love them I have too. Let's stand together as one if we do this the glory of God would rule the earth.

This was another hard period, not being with my family, watching them leave each time I saw them or each time I saw her. After so many visits and so much time spent together, next I heard from Jen, "Why don't you come out with us?" I asked my father-in-law, and he said, "You can come and spend the night." We hung out at my brother's house for the weekend, and when we went back, I stayed at her father's house for a couple of days. During that time, I was also attending anger management classes; from there I would travel back to Long Island. It didn't seem that hard after a while. God was making everything all right.

Between spending time at Jenny's father's house and spending time at my brother's house, we would ride the train to church. I was determined to get all of God; the train ride wasn't all that bad.

Before the incident in the apartment, God blessed us tremendously with the support of one of our sisters in the church to help us get a car.

Now, the car was parked up during this time, and God provided a way for us to get our car back. This was something we got excited about; it was our very own. We would ride that small Nissan everywhere. We would take weekend trips out to Jersey as a family; we stayed at the hotel, and then we would go to church. Eventually, we started spending more time together as a family. She started staying out on Long Island for a little bit. Remember when I told you there's always a ram in the bush? There was another ram in the bush. A friend of ours opened their doors up to us for a little while, and we were able to stay there for a couple of weeks as a family. I thank God. We thank God for that time, and we thank God for them. You never want to wear out your welcome, so when our time was up, God presented another opportunity: A family member of ours opened their house to us, and we were there for a couple of years.

Through detox, through people opening their doors to us and through people not wanting to open their doors to us, through people turning their backs on me, I've learned what to do and what not to do. I've learned through other people's behavior how I should behave. I just thank God that I went through what I went through. I have to reiterate: I did not do physical rehab, and I did not go through the process. I detoxed for five days; the rest was just God. THE REST WAS ALL GOD: me seeking Him, literally seeking His face and not just His hands. Me breathing in Him, Him breathing in me, and that's why I always say God never lets us go. In return, I grabbed onto God, determined never to let Him go.

I even remember that during one of my conversations with God, I told Him that if I'm doing this, being this person, living this way, wanting to live this drug-free lifestyle, don't give me my family back just because I want them back. That was very hard for me to say, but I meant that because in all my years of suffering with this addiction, God finally freed me.

Since I was a teenager up until the day that I gave my life over to the Lord, from the age of about 17 to about 44 or 45, I've had many nights of crying, asking God, "Please take this away from me. Please help me to get off of this. Please, God, I don't want to be this way. Please, God." I would spend these nights crying, feeling lonely, feeling abandoned, feeling left out, feeling like I wasn't a part of anything. I knew that people were putting me down, talking about me, thinking less of me. I felt like I was less than; I didn't feel like I was worth anything. Through all of that, I knew I wanted God. I have testimonies upon testimonies. I remember one time, when I was getting high in the street, somebody came up to me prophesying to me that I would be great in the kingdom of God. There I was, smoking and drinking around a bunch of my friends, and they said they saw me glowing. I would hold on to occurrences like this. I remember my aunt would always call me by my grandfather's name. My grandfather was a preacher, and his name is my second name. My full name is Richard David Kinard, so I am named after both of my grandfathers.

My aunt would always call me and say that I reminded her of my father's father, that I looked like him, that I acted like him, I moved like him, and he was a preacher. Even that would play in my mind; I would think, *Well, God is calling me*, and I've heard people saying, "God is calling you to a higher level," and so I gravitated to God. I desired to have Him more than my own family.

But God blessed me with my family anyway because, as I said in previous chapters, Jenny and I did not realize when we first started praying early in our relationship that these prayers would later cover us through the turmoil and struggle we would endure. God is on the move.

Dear Jennifer,
    You have been the only person there with me. Through it all you stood strong. Thank you I pray God bless you will the desirous of your heart/self

    If you wasn't there for me I might not have made it. You preys to God were answer, and that's why I am the man I am today. Your faith was enough for the both of us you kept praying and God hear. Maybe It wasn't in the way we wanted him to answer but he did.

    Out of everything that happen I see blessing. Our love is stronger and I have become a strong man in my faith. In time all thing will be restore and we will look back and say we made it over. Can't wait for that day to come. To hold you in my arm look in your eyes and say we have arrived.

    Jenny it's me and you against the world. If noone else tell you, you are a great woman. Sorry for all the wrong I've done. In time I will give you all the thing you always wanted from me. You already have my heart, mine, body and soul. Now I want to give you the worldly porsations.

Looking forward to a brighter better day. Everyday I seek the lord out, and he's show up in the lest Iunexected time. Today is a day when I feel every emition thinkable. But I am gonna keep on praying till I reach the highest ground.

Stay with me in spirit never let that love you have for me go. Together we are something to wrenckin with. Divide we will fall, God want us together to help someone. Our lifes is a testormine. Keep praying day and night my love we are winner.

Jen I see you in my future as I hope you see me in yours. Never fear there's no need to I am yours forever as long as you would have me. Let go of all negetive feeling and trust in God that he will complete the work he start in me.

"So if the Son makes you free, then you are unquestionably free."
— John 8:36 AMP

Jennifer: Deciding whether to stay or leave, and the moment I chose to either stand by his side through recovery or leave

How are we going to return to being a wholesome family after all this? Is it possible? The damage seemed unrepairable; so much hurt was caused.

Each time he walked out the door, I thought about whether to stay or leave. On any given night, I wasn't sure whether he was coming back home in an hour or at midnight — or if he was coming back home at all. I constantly thought about the whole plan I had in my head to pack the kids up and jet, but where was I going to go? I didn't have money to save. No one knew the whole truth. *Who's going to take me in? Who cares?* Who really cared, though? I mean, a part of me believes people knew he was on drugs. *Which family is going to take us in?* I guess no one would have taken us in unless I said something. But would they? I didn't know that, so I had nowhere to go. Truth be told, I didn't want people to know. I was too ashamed and fearful. I thought all these crazy things about myself. *Why tell anybody? What are they going to say? What are they going to do?* So this thought of leaving, wanting to leave, continued to exist. I think that day, when it all broke, I was left with little to no choice as shared in Chapter Three.

It all just came crashing down. I left my house and my husband, and we had nowhere to live. *What are we going to do?* I was really freaking out because I did not want this type of attention on any of us. People were outside watching and listening, seeing our family in uproar. We didn't live like this; we didn't like to draw attention to ourselves or make big scenes, but it happened. I was past the point of no return. So I left everything behind. Our girls used to have Barbie dolls, Barbie houses, Barbie everything, and I loved it for them. I didn't have that growing up, so I loved it for them even more, and all of it was left behind. Everything was left behind; we just got up and left. We took what we could, packed up and left the rest behind. Papers, documents, all gone, and we never went back. I learned that he came out of jail and went to live with his brother while I was with the kids. He slept on a couple of friends' floors and was homeless for a bit. Never thought it would look like this. Who does that? Who leaves an apartment fully furnished to go be homeless? But it happened, and so fast that I couldn't even process it. I didn't go to a shelter; we slept on people's floors, and sometimes we were blessed enough to sleep on a bed or a couch. Eventually, the kids ended up staying with a family member.

I was a homeless mom with three kids while Rich was living with his brother. I thought, *Well, he's living with his brother. He's good*, but I was trying to figure it out on my own with our three kids. I learned a lot during that time, like who to trust and who not to trust. But my kids went to school every day, and I still went to work. I still couldn't believe that this was happening, but it was and it did. It happened, and as time went by, Rich and I started to talk over the phone. I was able to yell, cry and express what he had done. I was telling him all about how he made me feel, and I don't think I even got it all out before he made me feel like trash.

As a woman and a mother, he made me feel less than; he made

me feel like a horrible wife, like I was nobody. I didn't deserve that. I was a good person, a good wife to him. I did everything I could think of to be there for him. I spent money, gave money and made sacrifices. I've been ashamed, been embarrassed, been spoken to in ways that I couldn't even believe. My life was destroyed. I felt like it had shattered into pieces, and I had no idea what to do with it. I felt like a fool. I felt like my mom was telling the truth. *My God, our two daughters watched their mother live through this. What in the world was I thinking? Oh, my God. I'm not a good mom.*

After it ALL, God still put us together. Deep down somewhere, I still believed, and I still trusted him, but I didn't know what God was going to do with us. The day before the incident that led me to leave the house with the kids was the day I went to church, gave my last and told God, "Whatever you do, just do it." After the incident, I had to ask God, "God, did You mean for it to be this way? Was I supposed to leave him? What's going to happen now, God? We have nowhere to live. We left it all behind." I was beating myself up for it and felt like a horrible mom because I put my kids through that process when I probably didn't have to. My kids didn't have to go through homelessness. I could have put him out, and I could have been living in an apartment with the kids. *Why didn't I do that? Why didn't I make him leave? Why didn't I believe in what God gave us?* I didn't know what the rescue was going to look like. *Oh, God, please forgive me if I did anything wrong.*

Rich and I started talking more and more, and then we eventually saw each other in person. I knew I loved him and had missed him. In one of our conversations, he said to me,

"Jenny, I told God, 'If I don't love myself enough or can't get myself together, then don't give me back my family.'" At first, I was crushed when he told me, but I understood what he was saying. I knew he meant it because I felt it with everything in me. When I heard him say that, and after I got over briefly feeling like he didn't want his family, I said to myself, *We're going to make this work.*

I stood by him all those years. Why not now? So I went back to my husband and stood by him. I knew we still had some ways to go, but I believed that it was going to be okay. Deep down, even though there were moments when I questioned it all, I still believed.

Don't get me wrong — I still believe Rich is a good person deep down. He has a big heart, but this ugly thing had latched onto him and didn't want to let go. I had to believe in God, and so I stood by my husband. Some people didn't like that I stood by him. Some people thought I was stupid for standing by him. I lost some people during that time, but all I knew was that I had to be the wife God called me to be and stand by him even in the middle of a separation. When I went back, it wasn't like, "Jen, you're trying to do this." It was like, "God, You got this now because I don't. I didn't then, and I sure don't now." I had no other choice but to depend on Him because standing by Rich's side was the decision I made with God.

"After you have suffered for a while, the God of all grace [who imparts His blessing and favor], who called you to His own eternal glory in Christ, will Himself complete, confirm, strengthen, and establish you [making you what you ought to be]." — *1 Peter 5:10 AMP*

CHAPTER 6

EARLY DAYS OF RECOVERY

Richard: The physical, mental and emotional struggles of early recovery

We had been living in Amityville for about a year. Jenny and I sometimes had to leave the house because I didn't want the kids to see me crying. We were living in a basement, and I remember hearing things like, "Oh, they're really not looking for a place to move or live." Little did they know Jenny and I would be on the computer every day looking to find a place to call our home. You know it is hard to hear someone you respect and admire doubt that you are doing what you say you are going to do. You know, it hurt us to hear that. So, as I said before, we would leave the house and drive around Amityville because I needed moments to get my emotions in check. We would ride down what we call "the strip," 110 in Amityville, and I would cry in the car. I would ask God, "Why are we here?" and "When are we going to get our own place?" This was one of the hardest times in my life, pleading with God, "Please move on our behalf." I would say, "I know I did wrong, and I know I messed up, but God, I'm trying. I'm working at living and working for You."

A few years into living in the basement, it became tense in the house. Our kids would hear the hurt in us, and as a result, there was a situation that arose in the house between two people. We knew then that we had to get out. So now, you're going to see God at work. An old supervisor from the last Head Start program I worked at became a supervisor at another Head Start program that I would eventually work for.

Here's what happened: It was a snowy November, and my old supervisor called me because she knew I had been looking for work. I wasn't able to work around kids because my police report said that I acted in a manner that endangered children due to the situation that happened with me and Jenny in our house when we were living in Brooklyn a few years prior. Anyway, I started working at this Head Start program, and they had to check my record. For some reason, I was already out in Brooklyn. I don't know why I was out in Brooklyn, but I know it started snowing that day. So, Jenny came, and she picked me up. While in the car, the snow really started picking up. Here go my emotions again. I was breaking down in the car, pleading with God: "Please, please, I need You to open a door."

I was like, "Man, God, I've been doing all I can."

I was bawling in the car, I was crying out to God, I was frustrated. I was like, "God, what's taking so long?"

Right then and there, my old supervisor called me. She said, "Rich, can you come over the weekend to shovel snow?" and I said sure.

Before I reached Long Island, I got another call from my old supervisor. She told me, "We're just going to hire you. You can come in and complete the rest of the paperwork."

So I started, and I worked there for about three weeks. God was starting to open doors now, guys. We had found this place before I got the job, but the landlord hadn't decided if he wanted to give it to us or not because we couldn't afford what he was asking for. This is why my emotions were so high in the car. Because I was like, *We found the place. God, now I need to keep this job so we can maintain the rent. I began to ask myself all these questions: How are we going to get this place? How? How are we going to pay for the security, the down payment?* All of this was playing in my mind, and I'm feeling helpless and praying everything works out with this job. While I was on the job, the landlord called us and said, "I want to give y'all the place."

The asking rate was the amount that we could afford. I remember that after getting the call from the landlord, I went into the kitchen where I work because the person in there, my coworker, was a believer. I went and told them. After telling them what happened, we started praising God together in the kitchen. I was working, and we were going to get this place, so I was happy. Right after I came out of the kitchen, I got a call to go into the director's office. There, she told me my background check came back. My work performance wasn't a concern, but they had to let me go.

I was crushed. I couldn't believe this was happening. I still had to trust God, but I didn't know what the next move would be. I knew something had to happen even though I lost the job;

for some reason, I had confidence. So the time came where we had to get the place for us to live. I didn't have the check — *Man, I don't have the money to pay for the place. Oh, my God, what is going on?* I had to wait on Him. I could have used the money I made while working at Head Start as the deposit for the place, but the check was not going to arrive on time for us to make the deposit. So then, I had to swallow my pride and ask someone to borrow the money until my check arrived. It was most uncomfortable for me, but we knew for sure that we needed this place; it was time for us to move on. I made the call and asked to borrow the money, and they blessed us by loaning us the money. I kept my word and paid it back immediately when I received my check.

We were able to get our place. Oh, man, just to walk into a place of our own ... This was the first time; we used to stay in a two-bedroom apartment in Brooklyn. The kids were so happy. When we first got married and had our first daughter, God promised us that we would have a house. He never said we would own the house. So when we walked into that place after spending years living in a two-bedroom apartment, staying on couches with people and living in a basement, we had to dress up to make it comfortable for us. It was a ranch home; our son had his room, our two daughters kept their room to share and Jenny and I had a big room to share. It was *ours*. We finally were back as a family, on our own, and I will never forget our first Christmas. We didn't have much because we had to use all the money we had to pay the security deposit for the place. We got a little Christmas tree and little Christmas gifts. It was one of the best Christmases we've had in ages, one of the best.

> June 24, 2010
>
> Sometimes we all do wrong, and turn away from God. But I know he never turns away from you. My mistakes in life took me to another place that I ~~pray~~ I never goto again.
>
> You have to stay the course and ride the wave of life. The battle is won ~~but~~ but the war continues on. We all are at war but because of Christ the emier has to flee. Stand there is nothing else to do. My faith is all I have and it is all I need.
>
> God restore my family, I have lost a job and the apartment. But as long as I have my family I'm ok. My love for them and there love for me help me make it though the day. It still gets rough at time but, I've become a strong man as days go by. "Pray is the key yes faith undock the door."
>
> So much pain I have cause just want those I hurt the most to feel joy.

I look back at that, and I can see God's hand. When you pray to God, and you ask Him, and you just don't think He's hearing you ... He's always at work. He's always making the way. He's always fixing it up, getting stuff ready, preparing it. His hand is always moving. He's always there. Within about two months of being in our new place, I started a new job. I remember a story in the Bible of a man named Saul who was on the road to Damascus and was blinded by light. His name got changed to Paul, and Saul was a naughty man. We know that story. He was bad, a persecutor of Christians who killed Christians. I kind of had an experience like that — I was knocked down and blinded. Then, God opened my eyes and showed me His light, His way, His love, and my healing process began.

I had various struggles during my early stages of recovery, but I kept going.

I remember there were times when I would be in the basement of my brother's house, and again, I was praying. I was fasting and reading the Word. I was in it; God was just dealing with me, just opening up my heart. You know, at that time, He wasn't saying much. He was just opening up my heart. He was pouring His spirit, just moving all in me. And He started cleaning me out, purging me. It was an awesome feeling. At that time, I had some struggles. I remember this one time when I slipped up. I had gotten high, and we were in the car. Of course, Jenny wasn't too happy, and I was kind of angry; I was like, "You can't just put a chain on me. I'm trying." I know I was wrong, but I slipped up. I fell short. We had a little dispute in the car, and I was going to get out. As a matter of fact, did — I got out of the car. She left me, and I came back to my senses. I asked her to come back and get me, and we got through that.

Weeks went by, and we were doing good. I had another slip-up, another little relapse, but again, God was already in. He knew that I was fighting, and He wasn't going to leave me this time. I was scared, but I didn't stay in that fear. I got back into my Word, I asked for forgiveness and I kept on pushing. I relapsed three times. If you fall or have a relapse, just get back on your horse. Don't give up. Don't beat yourself up. Don't throw in the towel. Keep fighting. Keep fighting. I'm a witness. This journey had its bumps, little hiccups or whatever you want to call them, and some people may read this book and go, "Oh, my gosh."

But to this day, I'm rolling with God. I believe in confessing, and this is my time of confession. Confession is good for the soul. The Bible teaches that a righteous man will fall seven times; you will hear more about this later in this book. Jenny used to travel out of state to work and attend various trainings, and at this time, I was working at Home Depot during Christmastime. I worked in the lumber and building department, right next to the garden department, where the Christmas trees were sold. Whoever worked in the garden department around the holidays would get big time tips. Jenny was out of town; by this time, the kids were old enough to take care of themselves.

On this particular day, I don't remember where the kids were, but I was feeling pretty confident in myself, and I decided to visit my old hangout spot. I said to myself that I would just have a few drinks, then I'd leave and come home. Well, a few drinks turned into me getting high. My middle child had given me some money to hold for her — with that being said, I had a nice pocket change. One of my friends and I went out and bought crack. Needless to say, I spent all the money, and I hit the pipe all night long. Early the next morning, I caught the J train in Brooklyn, the Long Island Railroad to Amityville. I was like, *Man, what am I going to do now? God, I spent all the money my daughter gave me to hold for her.* I knew: *If I go to work, when I arrive, I can go work in the garden department so I can hustle the trees and make the tips.* I made all my daughter's money back and some. That was God showing Himself once again.

God's Word says, "A righteous man falls seven times," but God will never leave you once He starts something in you. He's going to finish it without your help.

God protected my family, showing His love and His power in my life and toward my life. In our weakness, God's strength is made strong. Amen.

You are strong in your weakness. God's strength will make you strong. I stumbled three times during my recovery, but I was determined not to stay in my ways. I would not go back to that mess. I use the word stumble because the scripture teaches us that it is He who can keep us from falling. So though I may have stumbled, I didn't fall back down; I just dusted myself off and kept pushing toward the higher calling. I kept pushing toward that mark, and I kept running toward God. I didn't run backward. I didn't say, "Oh, well, I messed up, and I'm going to throw in the towel." That's what the old Richie would have done. But the new Richie that God created kept me seeking Him and kept me from beating myself up. So don't beat yourself up — if you fail, if you stumble, just keep pushing yourself.

> Yes sometimes mistake will happen but remember, he's in control. My life has changed for the better. As you can tell I really seek God. Putting him first and trusting that he will give peace to us all. I couldn't say that before but yes I know now and God is real.

"Now to Him who is able to keep you from falling into sin, and to present you unblemished [blameless and faultless] in the presence of His glory with triumphant joy and unspeakable delight, to the only God our Savior, through Jesus Christ our Lord, be glory, majesty, dominion, and power, before all time and now and forever. Amen."
— Jude 1: 24–25 AMP

Jennifer: Navigating my emotional turmoil while supporting his recovery

I've always been supportive, even when I probably shouldn't have. I realized later that I've always been an enabler. I was in the midst of what I can call a whirlwind of emotions, full of fear, anger, guilt, sadness and hope, not knowing if I was coming or going. There were days when I wanted to be happy and couldn't because I didn't know what to expect from Rich. Some days I cried and then found myself using laughter to cover what I was feeling. I'd find myself having conversations with people and crying on the inside. I would talk to people, not truly hearing them but instead internally dealing with all of these emotions in the midst of being a wife, being a mother to his children, being whatever else he needed me to be. I wasn't sure what to feel.

Being intimate with my husband didn't always feel right. I would ask myself, sometimes while being intimate with my husband, *Is this the man that I want? Is this the man that God had for me? Is it him? Who is he today?* I didn't know, but I couldn't say that out loud, and I couldn't act the way I was feeling. I had to pretend to be happy, the most painful and uncomfortable feeling I had to endure. I was concerned that if I showed anything else, it would have caused an argument. So I had to keep it all of my emotions in — *Don't show it, just hold it.* NO VOICE.

In it all, I had to be strong. I had to be a strong mother. I had to be a strong father, regardless of him still being in the home. He was still a father, a presence in the home. He played with the children; he did activities with them. You know, he was there, but he wasn't the father that I needed him to be for our children. He wasn't the husband I needed him to be, so I had to be what and who was needed in the home.

Most times I had felt as though I failed our children. Why did I keep them in this mess?

I did the next best thing, which was to talk to God for Him to help me come out of it. At this point, some of my emotions had led to making me feel depressed and like I could just end it all at any given moment.

Every day I went to work as if life was great at home. Depending on who I was speaking to, I would speak highly of him, not trying to let folks know what was happening. I thought I was protecting him, but I was too ashamed.

I asked myself several times, *Do you love him?* I never asked myself if I loved myself.

I just asked if I loved him. *Does he love me?* I thought about that and all these other problems that I had, but I never asked myself if I loved myself. Did I love myself enough to take care of myself? I tried to take care of myself, but it was difficult.

Nothing changed for him. *How can I live with this? How can I be me in the midst of this?* I was walking this earth so jacked up. Even when I called on God, my emotions ran me most of the time. I was fighting for my husband, fighting, praying, fasting and having little conversations with God, dealing with certain people — not many because I didn't let people in. Many times

I felt like taking my life. There were days when I just felt like running away because nothing I did was working, and I had to maintain who I was at the time so that my family could live. That's the mentality I had. I had to show resilience even when I didn't feel resilient. I continued to drown in all these emotions, not knowing what to do with them yet still supporting my husband, still being there, hoping for it all to turn around for the sake of our children and our marriage.

I had to believe no matter what I felt. I knew his recovery was his responsibility, but I also believed that we were all in this together, so I hung in there while carrying the weight. In all of this, I learned that healing isn't a destination but a journey — one filled with tears, prayers and moments of resilience I didn't know I had. While his recovery is his own, my strength in walking beside him has become my own victory.

"That, regarding your previous way of life, you put off your old self [completely discard your former nature], which is being corrupted through deceitful desires, and be continually renewed in the spirit of your mind [having a fresh, untarnished mental and spiritual attitude], and put on the new self [the regenerated and renewed nature], created in God's image, [godlike] in the righteousness and holiness of the truth [living in any way that expresses to God you gratitude for your salvation]." — Ephesians 4:22–24 AMP

CHAPTER 7

REBUILDING TRUST

Richard: Earning back her trust — acknowledging the harm I caused and working to rebuild

So I was building back trust with Jenny. It wasn't about me opening doors, being at home, giving her my money or my paycheck or doing any physical thing. You know what it was? It was her seeing my relationship with God — not me actually doing it so that she could see it, just me living righteously, living in a way where I'm seeking Him, chasing after Him, obeying God and living for God.

It began to resonate, and that's when our trust started building back because there wasn't anything that I could do physically or emotionally. It had to be done spiritually. A lot of times we think that we have to build back trust by doing things, by proving ourselves to people, and that that's all well and good, but I'm telling you that doesn't always stick; it doesn't produce real trust. The real trust is when you personally develop your personal relationship with God and begin to seek God. Then, all the wrong that you have done to that person will manifest, and you will be able to speak about the hurt you have caused. You will be able to articulate your apologies in the right way.

You will start moving in the right way and showing the right attitude.

Apologies are good. Once you ask for forgiveness from God, then you go to the person that you offended, and you begin to apologize and show your remorse.

Here it is; these are the many things I had to apologize to Jenny for. I had to take ownership for what I did: "Jen, I apologize for all the wrong I've done. I must confess to you with my own mouth and my own words. I was wrong when I took the money out of your purse; I was wrong when I took things to the pawn shop. I'm sorry for lifting my hands to you. I'm so sorry for that. I was wrong when I pawned the kids' computer games and my mother's ring that she gave you. I was wrong. I was wrong for staying out all night."

It's hard for someone to confess the wrongs they have done and admit them. When you truly admit it, it's hard. It hurts you; it brings a pain in you that you probably never experienced. Just saying sorry is not enough — you have to say sorry and say what you're sorry for, confessing the wrongs that you have done. I had to be specific in the issue: "I was wrong for cursing at you. I was wrong for leaving you and the kids alone at night. I was wrong for taking all our money and not paying the bills and not spending it on the rent and food. I was wrong that Christmas when the kids didn't get the gifts they used to. I was wrong." Saying that and hearing it for yourself, knowing that you were wrong, that's when the healing starts.

It all came through the relationship that I was developing with

God, my personal walk with God, and Jenny began to see that I was honest and being truthful, trying to be faithful to God and to our marriage.

There were things I had to apologize for, and I had to admit all my wrongs. There were things that she didn't know, and I had to work on myself for her to see the changes and feel like she could trust me again. I could say things, but I had to apply action to them too. I had to speak to her better than I used to, care for her better than I used to, show my love for God and more. After some time, she was like, "Oh, he's opening up." I had to open up and make myself vulnerable because there was a chance that maybe she wouldn't want to hear it. I felt there was a chance she could have walked away, even in the healing process, because she didn't know these things I had to open up about.

Having trust in God, I knew we would make it through, even with my confessions to her.

"If we confess our sins, He is faithful and just to forgive us our sins and to cleanse us of all unrighteousness." — John 1:9 ESV

Jennifer: The difficulty of trusting again — learning to forgive while protecting my heart

Why would I trust him? After all I had to endure — and so, because he's saying that he's no longer on drugs, I have to trust him now? I used to believe trust was like a sturdy house: built slowly over time, brick by brick. But addiction came like a wrecking ball, shattering my marriage and my family, which I thought were strong. As I looked at him, I wondered: *Can I ever trust him again?* More importantly, *Can I trust myself to forgive without losing my sense of safety?*

I felt like I was always looking over my shoulder, like for the next shoe to drop. I had some hope, a little bit, but I was always wondering because I didn't know when this thing was going to come back or if it would make a grand return. I mean, I saw and lived through the few relapses that he had, so it was hard for me to trust. I kept leading the family and trusting that something would happen quickly. I led the family for so long that I kept doing it and held tight to it because I did not feel like I could have let it go even when I knew that leading the home was not my role. In all honesty, at first, I did not realize that I was being untrusting, but when I realized it, I did not care. I did not want to let my guard down. I managed the money, managed taking care of the kids, and just made sure things were good in our home because I did not want to depend on him.

He started a job at Home Depot, and he was doing his part to contribute to the home, but I still did not trust him 100%. I was hiding money, selective about what to share with him. In all honesty, I would intentionally be that way, and other times,

I naturally flowed that way. We had the opportunity to move into our own home together as a family for the first time in a while, and even though Rich had a job and was making every effort to be a good husband, he was still in recovery mode and all my antennas were on high alert. However, it was a day-to-day process, but I always wanted to stay to protect myself from any unexpected issue that may arise. As time went by, trusting was hard, but I was trying my best to let my guard down slowly. Some years later, we eventually moved to Pennsylvania. I prayed and asked God for a certain type of husband. I said, "God, please give me a husband that loves me. Give me a husband that will chase after You; that alone would make me feel comfortable and safe. I don't need him to take care of me so that I can stay home and not work or do anything. No — I want to be a wife to my husband; I want to be his helpmate in any way needed. I want to be the wife that You call me to be, God, but I need him to be a husband to me. I need him to shield me and protect me. I need him to take this weight off of me so I'm not carrying it. I don't want to be at the head; it is not my seat, and I am most uncomfortable. But God, I don't trust my husband to hold this seat and lead this family. So, what do I do? I got to do this so we can all be safe."

But it wasn't my seat to hold, so stuff still wasn't right. Stuff was still a little shaky because I had to let go and let God continue the work that was already started. I thought I was letting God be in control, but I sure wasn't. One night while living in Pennsylvania, Rich and I had an argument. In the middle of the argument, he turned around, looked at me and said to me, with such fierceness in his eyes, "I'm not going back for you or nobody. I'm not going back to drugs for you or nobody. I don't want to argue; I don't want to fight." When he said that, a small part of me felt a little hurt. Now, why in the world would I feel hurt? You heard what this man said, right? That's not a bad thing, but I did, because I was like, *What about me?* That's how I felt for a moment. I made that thing about me for 2.5 seconds, but it wasn't about me. So I took a moment and reflected a lot on what he said. I'm like, *Jen, you heard that he's not going back for you or nobody. This man is serious about this walk. He's serious about not going back to drugs. He's serious about this.*

Jen, what did you ask God for? All these questions started coming to me: *What did you ask God for? You have to step back and let Him lead. Learn to trust this man. Let Rich lead; let this man take his rightful place. This seat is not yours. It wasn't yours from the beginning, and it's still not yours.* This was me talking to myself. I didn't share my thoughts with him at that moment. I believe I shared with him later on because I was embarrassed, telling myself, *He's been through all this. Why would you push buttons? Why are you not hearing what he's saying? What are you doing?* And so I started beating up on myself all over again. If I'm honest, I didn't let go right away. It still took me some time, but I was slowly getting it.

All these years, I thought I was better and that I totally trusted him in everything. Well, on October 18, 2024, I realized that I 100% trust this man. Yes — I came home with my pay stub, and I showed it to him. In all the years I'd been with my husband, I never showed him my pay stub — NEVER! I felt light and good after that experience. I was having a conversation with him, showing him my stub, listening to his direction about spending and saving, which I'd never done before. At that moment I realized, *There you go. 100%. Now you're 100% trusting him.* I didn't even realize I didn't 100% trust him before until that moment while showing him my pay stub. It blew my mind. I spent all these years having difficulty trusting him, but it was difficult to trust because look what happened. He stole from me. He spent my money, forced me to give him money, kept begging me for money, sold my stuff, sold the kids' stuff and pawned stuff.

How could I trust that? How could I feel safe with that? But then, in the same breath, I asked God to give me a certain type of man. God held his bargain, and I didn't hold mine. I didn't do my part.

I didn't fully forgive like I thought I did. Trying to forgive was a little bit difficult, because certain spotted moments kept coming back to my mind, and I was like, *How did he do this to me? Why did he do this to me?* But I had to keep remembering: *You've been talking to God, Jenny. You've been asking God for X, Y and Z. God loves you. God is in this. Trust Him. Forgive Rich, Jen; forgiveness is not for you.* I heard these things so many times during this process. I felt like I heard so many sermons during this process set up just for me, all about forgiveness. Maybe, probably, I wasn't trying to listen because I just didn't want to hear those sermons. I wanted to hurt him at times because of how much pain I felt.

But that wasn't what God wanted, and sometimes I felt like I was not falling in line like I thought I should have. This played a part in delaying a lot of things in our lives, aside from his drug addiction. I felt I didn't fully surrender to God; I didn't fully trust God. I said I did, but I for sure didn't demonstrate that trust. I already didn't trust Rich and had trouble forgiving him. I didn't let go; I said I did, but I really didn't, or I said I did, then went back and picked it back up. I did a lot of that with a lot of insecurities. But can you blame me? CAN ANYONE BLAME ME? I was supposed to just say, "All right, I forgive you. I trust you. Let's go lead the family," right there in that moment. That's what God wanted me to do. I didn't feel like I could do that because at that time, I never knew what I was going to face when I woke up the next day. I had to trust the words coming from the mouth of this man who, just a couple of months ago, was someone completely different. *How do you do that?* But eventually, I did, because I took my eyes off of myself. I took my eyes off of him, and I started looking at God. God knew it was going to take me some time, but I developed a willing spirit to get there. I didn't have it in the beginning; it was almost like it wasn't for real.

But God kept showing me: "You asked me for this, this and this. Can you see it?" Do you know why I couldn't see it? Because I was too busy looking at it with my natural eyes, and I did not allow myself to see it in a spiritual light. And when I finally did that, I was able to see stuff differently. I was able to speak differently. I was able to pray for him, without concern, without worry, knowing that God got this and He got Rich.

It wasn't easy. I had reached a space in my life and in our relationship where I felt like I had to protect myself. I had to protect my heart for the first time in a while. I wasn't beating up on myself too much, so I spent the time trying to protect myself yet I wasn't forgiving him and was still having trouble trusting him.

But somehow, *somehow*, with God, I was able to still protect my heart, still love Rich and slowly begin to trust him. You see, what the devil meant for evil or for destruction of my husband, God turned it for His good: "God intended it for good to accomplish what is now being done, the saving of many lives. So then, don't be afraid. I will provide for you and your children" (Genesis 50:20–21 NIV). God reminded me: "And we know that in all things God works for the good of those who love Him" (Romans 8:28). Slowly I started forgiving him. Slowly I started trusting Him, being in the process, letting it just flow and not trying to take control. Every so often, I had moments when I would — the flesh would flare up, you know — because I had triggers.

Back then, my husband didn't understand that certain things or movements he did were triggers for me, and I would find myself pulling back into that space of not trusting or not forgiving because I couldn't allow myself to get hurt anymore. I had to just pray to get myself out of that. I had to pray and keep talking to God. I had to trust God in this. I had to stay faithful. I had to believe that God would protect me and keep me. *Stay faithful, Jen. Don't let go; keep the faith, God got you. You do not have you. God got you. You cannot control this anymore. God got control. Let God be in control. Let God lead, Jen.* I had to have these conversations with myself. I couldn't have it with anybody else. Do you know why? Because I didn't tell anybody else the true things I was feeling on the inside — only God and I knew what those things were. I had no other choice but to talk to God; He brought me comfort, He brought me peace and He stood with me through this. God never sleeps, He never forgets, He never lets even one moment go to waste, He uses any and everything for His glory. No matter what I felt, no matter what I was or wasn't doing, God was working. I had to let go and trust God.

Trust takes time, and forgiveness takes courage. You have strength to rebuild, protect your heart and heal.
"Now to Him who is able to [carry out His purpose and] do superabundantly more than all that we dare ask or think [infinitely beyond our greatest prayers, hopes, or dreams], according to His power that is at work within us." — (Ephesians 3:20–21 AMP)

CHAPTER 8

THE ROLE OF GOD, COUNSELING AND THERAPY

Richard: How therapy changed my view on addiction and healing

Therapy for me looked different than therapy for the average person. I went to detox; I do remember I was reading the Word a lot. I would pray a lot while I was there because the food wasn't the greatest. I guess I was kind of forced to fast a little, and my communication with God was heightened. I would sometimes call my wife on the phone, and we would talk. It made me happy to hear her voice. Even though I went to detox because other people wanted me to do it, I'm glad I did it. It wasn't all that bad. I was able to dry out completely.

I was also mandated by the courts to take anger management classes for the incident when I elbowed my wife. This would last for some weeks. I don't remember too much about what was discussed in the classes, but I know that time in my life was still a struggle because mentally, I didn't want to do it, but I did not have a choice. Riding the train, I would think about God's goodness and what God promised me. I knew that what God had started, He would finish, He would complete, He would bring to an end. So I don't remember what we discussed in the classes, but I know that I completed the process, and I felt good about that. It gave me closure to some things. I didn't have to run back and forth to the court; they wouldn't be chasing me. That was done. Anger management might have helped me in more ways than one, and at that time I didn't realize it. It may have calmed me down, but I just don't remember what was discussed in those classes. It was so many years ago.

Throughout this journey, I had many talks with God. There was just something in me that was settled and said, *When God does it, it's going to be completed*. I'm not saying that this is for everyone. Some people may have to go to rehab; some people may have to get professional help. I'm not saying that you shouldn't — do all of that if you need to, but your main focus should be trusting in God and His power to heal, deliver and set free.

I also believe another part of my healing process was confessing my sins, talking to people about what my struggles were and what I dealt with. James 5:16 — this is the New Living Translation, which I love — says, "Confess your sins to each other and pray for each other so that you may be healed. The earnest prayers of a righteous person have great power and produce wonderful results." I am a living witness to these wonderful results. I'm a living witness to what confessing your sins to another can do. I'm a witness to its healing power. I'm a witness, again, to the great results of confession, prayer and healing. I believe that through that, most people will look at being delivered. I believe that you must be free, then delivered and healed. To complete the cycle and experience full evidence of God's power, you must have all three. You know, I've seen people who said they were delivered, but I believe that what they experienced is a combination of healing, deliverance and being set free because who the son sets free is free indeed.

"So if the Son makes you free, then you are unquestionably free."
— *John 8:36 AMP*

Jennifer: Couples therapy — how professional help saved our marriage and helped me heal from the trauma of addiction

We never went to professional therapy. It wasn't something Rich was interested in, so I never pushed the issue; all I had was prayer. But God also gave me a good friend during this process. We used to work together. We hung out together and spent a lot of time together, and she was one of a few people whom I was able to tell more than others. We became really good friends, and even to this day, we're still good friends. Our relationship got a little shaky when I went back to Rich, but we mended our relationship later on, maybe a year or two later. Even then, she was good to me throughout.

You know, I never thought about friendship being a form of therapy, but she was a good listener, and I was able to share. I was able to weep with her a lot. She didn't come in at the beginning of it all, but when she came into my life, I needed a friend. She was that person. I remember she drove me where I needed to go and picked up my kids. She was a great help, a great listener and a great friend, and I truly appreciate her presence during that time. I don't know what it would have been like if I didn't have her at that moment; I might have spoken to one or two other people, but I knew that I wasn't as open with others like I was with her. I was able to share a lot more with her, and I cried with her more than anybody else. I appreciate her being my sounding board during that season in my life. Folks have no idea how much I really appreciate that relationship, and I just thank God. I didn't have any direct therapy where I sat down with a therapist. Did I talk with my pastor? I did, and I wasn't fully honest; I didn't tell it all. I didn't tell all that was happening. I didn't tell what I was feeling. I held back some things and just told a little bit of the story, not all of it, because I was ashamed. I was trying to protect my husband and my family, and I was ashamed. I did not feel 100% safe in telling it all.

So I held back in some spaces, not saying everything, or not saying what was happening with me, or what I was feeling or whatever the case was at that time. So the little talks here and there with a couple of people were my therapy. Another part of my therapy was moments I got to myself where I could just talk to God. I could have gone to therapy for myself, but I didn't. I just felt like I just had to trust God since therapy wasn't something Rich wanted to do. I didn't think any further of it. I was just hoping and praying that this last thing would be the beginning of something great. I had to pray that all that I asked God for would come to fruition. That's all I had at the time. That was my therapy. That was how I spent my time. I read books and the Bible, I listened to songs, I listened to sermons, I listened to different encouraging tapes. I'd rewind, just keep playing and hoping.

After some time, we got together as a couple. We talked, but I felt like we didn't talk about everything. I knew I didn't share everything, like what I'd felt, what I was still feeling and what I was wondering. I didn't share those because I didn't want to hurt him or make him feel any type of way, especially when he was starting to make headway. Therefore, I just played it safe in the things that we talked about, and we didn't talk about some things when we should have. We didn't talk with the kids, and

I often wondered in recent years why we didn't hear from them once they were old enough to express their feelings.

Back then, therapy would have been important for the kids. We didn't do that for them, and I regret that today. A couple of folks suggested that we needed therapy, but Rich wasn't interested in that, and I honestly don't recall ever talking to Rich about it because I believed he would have said no. I don't think anyone said it to Rich that he and his family needed therapy. Even though I agreed, I knew that it wasn't something he was interested in at that time, and so we never went to a professional therapist. We just talked. We went to church Sundays and just kept trying to stay close to God. We started sharing a little bit of our testimony in church and to others, and that became our therapy. As time went on, we started sharing our testimony more and more. Richard had a strong belief that he should always confess his sins. At the time, he was like, "This is what God wants, and this is how we should be."

So he just started sharing some things. He would spill in front of people, and I would be like, *Why is he telling people this?* I was somewhat embarrassed, but he always said to me, "Jen, we got to do this. I got to do this, and this could probably help somebody else. I have to confess; I have to tell it."

And so that's how he started being that way, just telling it out there to anyone and everyone. At first, I thought he was bugging, but I got used to it. Looking back now, maybe that was his form of therapy; it felt therapeutic for me when I told my story to people. God created opportunities for me to encourage others by telling my story to people one-on-one, sharing what happened, sharing where we are now, sharing what we've been through, sharing that we're still in the process, but we're coming out, we're going through it together. I was most comfortable sharing with people that way, and it was very therapeutic for me, but I also started seeing that it was helpful for the person who was listening as well. And so those were my forms of therapy, nothing on a professional level. We didn't have that at all. My husband might say something different about how he handled that phase therapeutically, but for me, this is how it was, and it helped me a lot.

Did it help faster? I don't know. Sometimes I would fall back into wonder and concern, but sharing with others helped save us during that time, and we know that the number one person was God. Sharing our testimony and our trials with others — whether in the church in front of however many people or one-on-one, which worked best for me — was therapeutic. My moments spent alone with God, in communion with Him, were therapeutic for me. Those are mine. After some time, I became comfortable sharing with more than one person. I used to share at the school where I worked — not in-depth, though, because the students were young men. I was able to share some things with them. When they looked at me, they just thought I had it all, but I had to share with them: Mrs. Kinard *didn't* have it all. I shared a snippet of my story, which was therapeutic, and I learned from the young men that it was helpful for a couple of them. I'm grateful for those moments. Those moments were therapeutic, even if not on a professional level. To this day, I still use songs of worship; they're soothing and relaxing to me. Now that my husband and I are in a way better space, we're able to talk more openly than we could in the past. I am grateful for all of those therapeutic moments that I had while being in my marriage as my husband worked through this process.

"Heals the brokenhearted and binds up their wounds [healing their pain and comforting their sorrow]." — Psalms 147:3 AMP

CHAPTER 9

STAYING SOBER, STAYING STRONG

Richard: Strategies for maintaining sobriety, dealing with temptations and finding purpose in recovery

As I stated earlier, I had a few setbacks, but my objective was to stay sober and hang on to Jesus. I had to change my mindset. I had made up my mind to stay focused, and I knew that what God started, He would complete. So God created some willpower in me, and I was determined to live for Him. I'll never forget what God brought me from and carried me through. I'll never forget how I prayed to God in those times. I would ask Him to take this thing from me: "HELP ME! I don't want to be this way."

I would picture where I was, what I wanted and where I was going. Just seeing those particular things in my mind kept me from wanting to return to my old ways of getting high.

I wanted to live for God and to be in my right mind. When you're on drugs, you're living in a haze; your thoughts are clouded. I didn't understand that. I used to say to myself, *Oh, no, your thoughts aren't clouded*, but because I was using drugs, I could not see that my thoughts were indeed clouded. Now I have a free mind to see things with clear eyes and clear thinking, without so much of an "I guess" mindset. I now see myself how God sees me, and I understand how God wants me to be. Every day I would wake up, read a scripture, listen to my gospel and meditate on where I was, where I came from and where I was going. In my meditations I would remember when I was doing drugs, the places I was in and the pain I caused my family. My heart would feel like it wanted to jump out of my chest.

Thinking of those situations kept me sober, sane, stretching, reaching and chasing God. Not only have I stuck to this; I've stuck to the scripture even to this very day. **"Who the son sets free is free indeed."** When God puts His hand on something, it turns out better than when we put our hands on it. God knew us before we existed; to me, that means He knew who I would be right now. He knew all my trials, He knew what I was going to go through and He knew I was going to be struggling with this drug addiction. I stand today to say this is what keeps me sober. Sober is the term the world uses; I would like to say I've been delivered and set free. **1 John 4:4 KJV states: "Ye are of God, little children, and have overcome them: because greater is he that is in you, than he that is in the world."** God is in me. He did it for me.

I'm going to give you two short stories. When we first moved out to Pennsylvania, I was working for this company. We would clean out homes that were foreclosed by the banks or abandoned, and we did all kinds of repairs. It just so happened that a particular coworker of mine had just come out of rehab; he was strung out. He was addicted to dope, and he also smoked crack. We would be in the truck, and to be honest, we would talk about the crack and how we used to smoke it. He still had the hookups where he could still get crack, and he would be like, "Man, we could just go get some right now." I would say, "Aye, bet! Let's go get some," but I was just joking around. Readers may say, "Why would he joke like that?" I say to them: I am secure in who I am and even more secure of who God is in my life.

My mother would say to me, "Never say never," but in this case, I'm going to say it: I never want to go back — never. After telling him I was just joking, I told him I would never do drugs again, I never want to go back to that life and I would never go back to that life. I would use my life as a testimony with him, trying to tell him, "Listen, you know, you should think about getting to know God." I would ask and say things like, "Why don't you go to church? You should get to know God. That's what helped me stay sober."

Just a few years back, I had a buddy of mine sitting in front of my house. I was working at another company as a glazer, installing windows. A younger guy would call me his mentor; I was like a father figure to him. I remember he told me that he had a drug problem. He said he sniffed coke, and I had to tell him: "Hey. Listen, man — if you're going to be doing that, you can't be part of my life." I didn't feel that I would slip up and do it, but I didn't want to have that around me. I didn't want to open a door or put something in front of me that I knew would be an issue for me. I don't care how long it's been — I don't think you should ever put yourself in a place like that, so I had to tell him. To God be the glory; he just put the coke down. I guess our relationship was more important to him.

Those are just some of the things I experienced, and now I'm truly finding what my mission and purpose is. I'm telling my story and trying to bring people to healing in God. God is the truth, the light and the end. Through Him, you can be freed and delivered.

"So do not fear for I am with you; do not be dismayed, for I am your God. I will strengthen you and help you; I will uphold you with my righteous right hand." — Isaiah 41:10 NIV

Jennifer: How my role evolved — supporting his sobriety while also nurturing my own healing and self-care

If I'm honest, I don't think I allowed myself to heal 100% during the beginning stages of Richard's sobriety. I supported him, I was there for him, I was always a listening ear and I was there to pick him up after a couple of setbacks he had.

I just wanted him and the kids to be good, and I thought less of myself a lot during this process. I was on go all the time; I kept going, kept going, and kept going.

Even in those beginning stages, I was still operating in a role that wasn't designed for me: the head of the household. I eventually had to surrender that role.

At this point, Rich was no longer smoking weed or doing drugs. Yes, he had a couple of setbacks, but then he had to deal with finding a job — keeping in mind that when he got arrested, it was listed on record that he couldn't work with kids anymore, and he used to work at Head Start around children as a custodian. So he was trying to do better, and he was home. He didn't have a job, and he was watching his wife wake up in the wee hours of the morning to get on the Long Island Railroad to head out to Jersey. I was either driving out to Jersey in the wee hours of the morning or taking the train while he was home. He was a stay-at-home dad, but he had odd jobs to do here and there because he was good with his hands. He is a handyman and a plumber, and he was also capable of doing construction, so he got little jobs here and there while trying to step back into the role of leading his family.

While seeking a job he often thought, *Man, I can't go work with kids anymore because of the previous incident and my arrest. This has damaged my life*, hence why I led the family financially at the time. I had to be an encouraging and motivating wife while staying focused, even when I felt inwardly tired.

Rich eventually got a job, and that helped pick his spirits up. He was determined to go through this walk without going back to where he once was, so my role evolved.

I went from not feeling depressed anymore to somewhat still sailing in the space of leading the home. I still didn't 100% trust Rich. I was still a little shaky, but I supported my husband nonetheless. I couldn't let folks talk about him. I still protected him; after all he was still my husband. I would inwardly say to myself, *He's going to beat this*, yet somewhere deep down in my stomach, I was still shaking, saying, "Please, God, please, God, please keep him focused."

Moments to myself were very rare, and when I had them, they were spent talking to God because I needed strength. I needed God to cover Rich. I needed God to keep him and my children. I have one son, and he couldn't have had this addiction fall on him. I had to shield and protect everybody except myself. I did a poor job of taking care of myself. I wasn't filthy; I was able to upkeep myself the best way I could at the time. There were a couple of friends of mine who gave me clothes because I wasn't able to shop for the kids during that time; they gave me clothes for myself too, and I had no shame in that. I wore the clothes proudly and appreciatively.

I believed in God for my family and for my husband, and somehow, I neglected myself. I just kept my focus on my family and held on to God to just keep us together. We weren't in our own space at the time. I asked God numerous times to bless the family member who kept our kids for some time, then allowed me and my husband to come join them and live in the basement. We made the best of it, and that was the most grateful season of our lives because we were back together as a family, even though we weren't in our own home together. We didn't care about that; we were just grateful. We didn't care if we slept on the floor or the rooftop. Just getting to be together as a family was a blessing.

I still found myself crying, but I wasn't crying out of fear anymore. It was just a mixture of emotions, and I'm sure I needed self-care and therapy during that time, but I didn't think about that for myself. I just wanted to protect my children and my husband. I was in a role that, like I said, didn't belong to me. I'm a mother and a wife, so I think my job is to protect my kids and my husband in ways of prayer against anybody who's speaking negatively against them. I've had people assume the worst of us. I've had people think that I was playing them because I would beg or ask to borrow money, and they thought I had it because they saw how I dressed, not knowing I was dressing that way because somebody gave the clothing to me. Those were some things I had to deal with mentally. I never really spoke out loud about it, but I didn't let that hang over me too much because I had bigger things — my family — on my mind. But people were being people, even the saints of God.

Even during all of those times before living in the basement, the beginning stages of his surrendering, stopping the smoking and so forth, God blessed us with shelter, with a family that took us in even when my husband was staying with his brother. That was the biggest blessing ever because he wasn't on the street. This could have looked different. My kids could have been called off to someplace, but they weren't. God shielded and protected us even in the midst of it all, so even though I didn't take care of myself, God somehow took care of me because I'm still here. I'm still standing.

Some might say, "You should have gone to therapy, and you should have done better." Well I did not, and I already stated why that didn't happen. But no matter what, I believed in God through it all, even in my moments of weakness. I still believed in God even in the moments when I was talked about. I still believed in God even in the moments when I didn't tell the whole truth of what was happening to me, with me, about me, about my family. I still believed in God when my children were fighting at times. God still had us. God still had me. Somehow, through all of this, God kept me, and I'm so grateful. I'm so grateful to God.

God said in His Word,
"My grace is sufficient for you [My loving kindness and My mercy are more than enough — always available — regardless of the situation]; for [My] power is being perfected [and is completed and shows itself most effectively] in [your] weakness. Therefore, I will all the more gladly boast in my weaknesses, so that the power of Christ [may completely enfold me and] may dwell in me." — 2 Corinthians 12:9 AMP

CHAPTER 10

REDISCOVERING LOVE AND INTIMACY

Richard: How recovery helped me become a better partner

Once I began to open up and became free from my addiction to crack cocaine, I went back to recapturing our first friendship. When Jenny and I first met, we were best friends, and I know that may seem like a cliche, but it is what it is, and it was what it was. We were cool. We would hang out; we would have long talks as friends, and I liked spending time with her. When we started dating, we spent a lot of time together, and she was that person for me. We talked more, laughed more, played games together, watched movies and talked about God all day long. We would study together, recapturing what we had — even better than before, like it was all new.

During my drug addiction years, I had lost all of that. I stopped listening, and I stopped wanting to spend time together. I would think about all she had said, but it didn't matter back then. Now, I look forward to hearing her voice more than anything else.

Me coming out of that must have drawn our relationship closer because now I don't really need people around. Back in my drugs years, all I wanted to do was hang out with the guys, smoke, do drugs and drink, but now all I want is to spend time with my wife. I enjoy her company. I enjoy the way she laughs, and we love to travel together. In our marriage, I don't need drugs or to hang out and get into things that don't honor God and our marriage. We have fun together. I love the God that's in her, and I love how she loves me.

I love holding her, holding hands, watching a good movie. I love to pick her up, which she doesn't like because she's scared of heights. So we wrestle, and when I try to pick her up, we struggle and, you know, one thing leads to another. Ha-ha.

I love being with her and in her presence, and please know that this is not made up. I love that woman. After all we've been through, she stood by my side. If nothing else, I fell in love with her all over again, stronger and better. What else is there to say when you can just spend time talking, holding each other, looking at each other, gazing into each other's eyes? It may seem cliché, like I said, but it is what it is. I'm glad we can share these moments. I'm glad we had God with us, knowing that we're not by ourselves. I'm glad we regained our intimacy, the romantic part of our relationship, which has heightened. When I'm at work, I call Jen. I say, "I just wanted to hear your voice" — or I might put a twist on it, "I just wanted you to hear my voice." We make each other laugh. We were doing some of this during my drug addiction years, but it wasn't the same, nothing like it is now.

We kiss each other goodbye each day, and when we return home, we kiss each other. We constantly let each other know that we love each other. Even in the times when we get upset with each other, we do our best not to let it keep us from each other. We get over things quickly, talk them out and move forward. We never did this during my drug days,

We firmly believe in not going to bed angry. We work hard on not living in a space of anger and frustration with each other for a long time. It happens, you will get upset with each other, but days cannot come between us being that way at all. Scripture teaches to not let the sun set while you're still angry. Holding each other doesn't have to be sexual; there is intimacy in holding her, hugging her, looking into her eyes, letting her know she's safe and so much more. Those are awesome moments, appreciating one another, looking at what we came from and, for me, just not wanting to ever put her into that experience of hurt again. My goal is to make her smile every day that we're together, even in our hard times, even when we have little disagreements. My goal was to come back, and I got to put a smile on her face. I love Jenny, everybody. I don't just love her — I'm in love with Jenny. *I'm in love with Jenny.*

I want to encourage somebody out there to find the thing you're in love with alongside your significant other — for us, it was God. When I say significant other, I'm talking about your spouse, not a boyfriend or girlfriend, not somebody you are just living with. See the power of God in our relationship and how God has brought us together, infused our hearts together to be one with each other and then to love the number one. We share Christ. We share Christ in our relationship. We share Him, and through Him, our bond and our relationship are growing. Our intimacy is growing. It's special, and that's what's unique about us. Our intimacy is special.

"Above all, love one each other deeply, because love covers over a multitude of sins." — *1 Peter 4:8 NIV*

Jennifer: Rebuilding emotional and physical intimacy after addiction strained our bond

Our love for and intimacy with each other during this stage of the relationship were like the bubbles in a sparkling cider drink that tickles your nose, with smiles and the interest of wanting more.

The love for each other has always been there. Even when the moments were hard, even when the hurt and disappointment were at the center of our relationship, even through tears, anger and frustration, our love still existed. Strangely enough, it did, and we're still holding strong. Even when I had moments of hate, love still existed. I knew that my love for God and my love for my husband kept me knowing what God wanted from me and kept me in those moments back then. Maybe it looked and felt like it's what Rich wanted, but it's always what God wanted. I wanted my husband to be better, and I put my hands all up in it, but I wanted to please God. With all the emotions that I went through, all my frustrations, all my thoughts, my mental breakdown and the lack of love for myself, I still loved him, and God was still faithful. We went through all of that, and we got to the space where Rich was able to go through his recovery phase.

The recovery phase did not last as long as the strong addiction phase. It had its highs and lows. This might sound bad, but there were moments where I was like, *If he's a little bit tipsy today, then I can probably get what I want*, and I did. I thought like that for a long time, but it didn't always work. But there we were, and he was in recovery, and at that point in our lives, intimacy didn't look well either; it didn't feel great during the time of his addiction. I faked the funk!

When we were intimate, nine times out of 10, it was because he wanted to be, and so I felt like I had to. Even when we were, I just felt like I was just there. I just pretended to be there. We used to have intimate discussions and conversations; it almost felt like we were dating all over again, and I had a great feeling of hope. The beginning stages of his recovery, when I started going to visit him in Long Island, were really good times. Even as I'm writing it now, I'm smiling about it because I remember the first time I went to visit him in Long Island, we were both happy to see each other. We made love with each other, and I didn't fake the funk! We spent a lot of time talking and just holding each other, and those moments felt great. They were moments of hope and a glimmer of light was ahead. It may sound as if I doubted his recovery, but I felt hope. I felt like we were getting somewhere, and as time went by, we had a lot of intimate conversations. We started to be more open with each other during that stage of Rich's recovery than we were during the addiction phase as newlyweds. I know I wasn't 100% open, but I was more open than I was in the early stages of our marriage. This was the beginning of something.

He did a lot of listening. He told me while he was in detox that counselors told him he had to hear me, so I was able to say my truth when we first talked over the phone. I was emotional and mad and everything at that time, but the intimate times we later shared — trips we made to Jersey just because, night or weekends in a hotel with or without the kids — played a big role in healing our relationship.

I rendezvoused at a hotel in Brooklyn, and nobody else knew. It was just me and him as planned. We were fully married, and here we were sneaking around, just creating time together, just being with each other. I enjoyed those times; they were spontaneous, and I didn't have that during the addiction phase of our marriage.

While he was on drugs, he had no problem being spontaneous with those damn drugs. I don't even know if they call that being spontaneous, but that was that. Us having intimate moments and time together like that — meet up here, go there — was pleasing to me.

The beginning stages of rekindling what we had were great — *HOPE HAS ARRIVED!* Do you even understand what it is like to make love with your husband while he's high — what that looks like, what that feels like? I felt like crap most of the time, but I didn't feel like I could have said no. There were moments when I didn't want to, but who wants to argue about that? Who wants to tell their spouse no to intimacy? There was a time when I did say no and stood firm in my no, and that caused an argument. I think that during that time, I was just getting tired of saying yes, and I didn't want to because I didn't know who was making love to me. I didn't know who was holding me, and I felt dirty. I didn't feel like a wife; I felt like I was just there.

The recovery phase was spent getting to know each other. It felt like a boyfriend-and-girlfriend type of thing, dating each other all over again. It felt good. Talking on the phone for long periods of time reminded me of before we got married;

we used to be on the phone for so long, just talking. It gave me hope, and I felt like I was getting my husband back and better. God answered my prayers, after all these years of living under a dark cloud that put a strain on our marriage, to be in the state where we were going through recovery and getting to know each other. Intimacy looked and felt different; it felt great, it felt exciting, it gave me a sense of hope that we were heading in the right direction — and not just because we were making love.

No, that has its place, but we were able to talk time and time again and be open. Even though I still wasn't open all the way at first, I was open more than I used to be. It still gave me hope, and I appreciated that recovery time in our lives, those moments, those memories, those glimmers of hope. Yes, he may have had relapses during his recovery, but I still believed. I still believed in God, and I still believed in Rich. I knew God had something for him. It wasn't easy — absolutely not. But I knew God was in the midst, and so in every moment of stumbling blocks — the 2.5 seconds of setbacks he's had during recovery — God was there. It wasn't great then, but we got through it, and we continued getting to know each other, spending more time together and sharing intimate moments together, just rebuilding what we had and getting to an even better space than before. It was almost like that old part of our lives died away, and here we were, starting new life together. Now the Lord God said,

"It is not good (beneficial) for the man to be alone; I will make him a helper [one who balances him — a counterpart who is] suitable and complementary for him." — *Genesis 2:18 AMP*

CHAPTER 11

OUR NEW LIFE TOGETHER

Richard and Jennifer: How our relationship has changed — becoming stronger through the shared experiences of addiction and recovery

Our new life together. We want to pause for a minute because we are about to take a turn in this chapter. Sit back and get ready to read our dialogue about our new life together and how our relationship has changed and become stronger through our shared experiences of addiction and recovery:

Jennifer: Richard, in what ways has facing addiction together strengthened our bond?

Richard: Jen, it's kind of like the road we've been on, or the road we've taken, I believe we were prepared for it. Like I said, we began our relationship praying together, and those long talks before we were married are the glue that held us together. It was as if God knew our journey before it happened, and He equipped us. The Scripture teaches us that God knew us before we were in our mother's womb. So, I think that's just the journey we had to go through. He strengthened us for everything that came after. Jen, that question comes right back at you.

Jennifer: Sure. I want to say that because we were in this together from the start, somewhere deep down, there was a spirit of determination. We were determined that we would not be apart. I remember we used to have conversations about never getting divorced — we would never do this, we would never do that — and we were serious about that, so it wasn't just talk for us. We lived that out. So yes, we had the period of separation, and yes, it was because of the drugs and so forth, but deep down, we both knew that there's a strength that lies. I know you love to talk about the way we started dating or courting each other on the phone, with long conversations and prayer, and I agree that yes, that sealed us. And yes, that determination that we have to stick together no matter what — we didn't know what was going to be in the future, and now we show that we are stronger than we were before.

Richard: Babe, this is some awesome stuff. People may not believe we're conversing right now, as this chapter is our conversation pieced together while sharing our perspectives. We're here, sitting in our spot, in our living room, in our loveseat, together, sharing this dialog. I want to ask you a question, Jen: How has our communication changed since we started working to do recovery together? From my perspective, I think that as we talk more, our conversations are different.

Jennifer: I feel a little bit more bold or confident in communicating with you about things. I don't think I shared this with you, but this was a recent event. I don't think I'd ever shown you my pay stub in all the years I worked. (For the readers, you've probably seen this in one of the chapters.) I don't think I'd ever shown you one of my pay stubs in all the years we'd been married, and it had been 31 years. I realized that a while after showing you my pay stub for the first time in the middle of the week, in the third week of October 2024. It hit me later on that I'd shown it to you. All I could do was give God praise for change. Showing you my pay stub and having financial conversations weren't things we did while you were on drugs; that wasn't a conversation at all. But now, our conversations about finance, our conversations about growing in Christ, our conversations about just communicating better with each other … We talked about listening to understand and not listening to respond and trying to practice that. We weren't doing that before we were in recovery; it was a hit-or-miss. And now, it seems like it's been a steady flow. Rich, you tell me, how has our communication changed since we started working through recovery together?

Richard: I don't know if we've had any laughter in this book yet, guys, but did you catch what she said? She never showed me her pay stubs. I never realized that. And here's the thing: I've been drug-free for a little over 10 years now, and she just now said this out loud. Wow. I never thought about that, nor did I recognize that. It took me a while — ha-ha. Jen you brought up a couple of good points. It's true; I always heard her when she spoke back then. I heard her during my addiction, but not enough to respond in the way she wanted because drugs were my priority. Her words stayed with me throughout those times, and I would share with Jenny how those words were still with me. I would tell her, "I'm listening to you." Jen used to say, "Listen to understand, not respond." She put that in me, and that became one of my calling cards. I tell everyone in this house that we practice listening to listen to understand, not to listening to respond. So in your relationship, brothers, you can listen to your wife. It doesn't mean that you're less than a man. They're not taking our title of being the head of the household; they're our support. They're here to be our helpmates. They're here to cover us like we should cover them. Our communication has grown because we can listen to one another.

Jennifer: So Richard, here's our last question of dialogue: How can we continue to support each other's growth and maintain a healthy relationship?

Richard: Simple, guys: Prayer. We have to pray for one another because once I'm praying for her and pushing myself aside, God's going to respond to that. When she prays for me, she's pushing herself aside. God's going to do what He said He will do for her. I pray that God continues to work in her life. I say something like, "God, I pray that You would just use my wife and fill her with Your spirit and bless her. Go to the fullness of her capabilities." By me saying that, in return, God is going to give her what she needs. By me praying for her, God is going to make her be what I need. Jen, I guess the same question is for you: How can we continue to support each other's growth and maintain a healthy relationship?

Jennifer: Well, you already mentioned prayer, but I think holding each other accountable is a big one. We may have tried to do that during our period of addiction, but that was a challenge because I couldn't control that, even though I was trying to control or to make you stop in so many ways. But now, as we are growing in our new life together — and I love to just hear the words "new life together" — I want to say, holding each other accountable so we can be better and stronger together in this relationship. You know, the prayer seals it. And if we fall short, if we mess up, it's okay for our spouse to say, "Hey," whatever the case may be, and we can hear it without being offended. Hear it from a space of growth. Hear it because they're trying to help you be better. I knew back then, when I was speaking so much and saying, "Rich! You got to stop, Rich," it wasn't being heard because this is what you wanted to do. But now that we are in our new life together and we are determined, we continue in our determination to grow. Holding each other accountable is a great way to go, coupled definitely with prayer as you mentioned.

Richard: Jen, that's great stuff. You know, as you were saying that, I started looking at you. Sometimes God downloads things, and I have to notice you. I have to notice when you're bothered by something. I got to notice when you're happy or sad. I got to notice these things, and I have to pick up on them, especially when you need me. We believe in celebrating when we have our victories and even before we have them, but there are times when I know I have to come into the house and show more affection and be intentional with it. This is not to say I don't; I just want to show it more — and guys, I'm still learning to be that physically affectionate, emotional guy. I have to be better at that. I have to get it. It has nothing to do with me being macho; it's just that I'm not used to it because of all the years of me not showing her that affection. I have to embrace my sensitive side. My wife is my queen — yes, she is my queen. My wife shares my vision. My wife shares my thoughts. My wife and I, we are one. God always interjects. When she shares things and I show rejection, God shows up and tells me, "Nope, she's right.

Do it that way," and the same for her as well. We've learned to humble ourselves to each other in this new life together.

We have to be aware of our surroundings. Our circle of men, we have to get in touch with our sensitive side and know that there is nothing wrong with that. That's why we stress listening. You have to listen. *Listen.* In this day and age, this world, everyone wants to respond and give their opinion on everything. Everybody's got an opinion on something. People, start listening to understand. Be quiet and listen and stay humble. Our Bible states: "My dear brothers and sisters, take note of this: Everyone should be quick to listen, slow to speak and slow to become angry" (James 1:19 NIV).

Well, we hope you enjoyed this chapter. We just wanted to have a little conversation and share our perspectives on different things, our answers to the various questions that we shared, which surround the change in our relationship and us becoming stronger through our shared experiences of addiction and recovery. We hope these questions and responses encourage you and give you a little insight on our relationship as to where we are in our new life together.

"Be completely humble and gentle; be patient, bearing with one another in love. Make every effort to keep the unity of the Spirit through the bond peace." — Ephesians 4: 2–3 NIV

CHAPTER 12

EARLY DAYS OF RECOVERY

Richard and Jennifer: Words of hope and encouragement for those in the midst of addiction or in recovery — reminding readers that healing is possible, both individually and as a couple

Richard: Hey, Jen. It's time we let someone know they're not alone. I feel God pushing us at this point of the book to encourage someone that they're not alone.

Jennifer: Yeah, Rich, I agree with you. You know, when we were going through it, I felt like we were alone, but we weren't. And so, with that being said, anyone that's out there, we know that they're not alone. People feel like they're alone because they feel like they can't tell their story or tell what's happening in their marriage or their home, whether it's due to fear of how people may look at them or something else. The whole experience could just make them so isolated, like we were. We were isolated to some point, you know? And people feel like they're alone because they don't trust. They don't want to put their stuff out there, right? Like, what do you think about that?

Richard: You know, it's always the man who's on drugs and

the wife. It's always the husband who's on drugs, and it's the wife who has to put up with it. So I want to change it and say it could be even the wife who's using and the husband who's struggling with seeing his wife go through this. Whichever way it lands, I encourage the person who is the stronger of the two to stay praying. In our situation, it just so happened to be Jenny. She was the stronger of the two of us, and even though we felt alone, I believe that her praying brought in such a presence that kept our union glued together.

We said this a few times in the book, but I believe we know that God was keeping us together with the way we started off talking to each other, the way we were when we were dating and the times we spent together. I mean, we didn't know the purpose for all of that, but we both believed that was what sealed it for us. We didn't know what we were about to encounter in our lives, but then it happened. Did we get weak at times? Did we get frustrated? We did, sure enough — sad days, sad nights, angry nights. All these different emotions happened: mad at the world, mad at people when we heard what they were saying about us or whatever the case may be. It happened, and we just want to say to whoever gets ahold of this book that we know you're not alone, and we understand the fear that you may have of not wanting to tell people. Tell somebody. I used to say to myself "Rich, you got to figure this thing out."

Because I was *addicted*. I was addicted hard; the book can't put you into where I was. There was a time when I knew my wife didn't know where I was a lot of nights. There were nights when I snuck out while she was sleeping. I lived on the fourth floor, so I would crawl. I would climb up the ladder and go through the roof, put the roof down slowly and go down through the fire escape, doing crazy things like that. That's how it was. But I felt the presence. You know that you're protected when you do stupid things, and they don't come back to bite you. You know that there's somebody. So when I would sober up, I would remember my actions, and I would be like, *Well God had to be with me.* I know it may seem weird or contradictory to people. Don't listen to the outside noise. Don't listen to those people who judge.

Listen to your heart. Find your heart. And I know it may seem crazy, like, "How can a crackhead find a heart?" If you've never smoked crack and you don't know the feeling, just don't comment. I'm speaking to that person who's struggling with this addiction. By talking to you, I'm showing you that you're not alone. I'm talking to you as you're reading this book and struggling with the addiction to crack cocaine. I'm pointing out that you are not alone. Listen to your heart. You reading this is proof that you are not alone. I'm talking to you. Whoever you are, grab a hold of your heart. That inner man is God, that piece that's saying, "Hey, I love you. Hey, I'm here for you."

You know that voice that you hear from deep down inside you? You know that feeling? That's God telling you you're not alone.

Jennifer: So true, even if you're a person who doesn't know Christ, right? We have people who will read this book who haven't accepted Christ, and we hope that you will come to know what eternal life is after reading this book even if you don't accept Christ. I haven't been on drugs, right? I haven't been on drugs.

Richard: Jen, can I interject here?
Jennifer: Go ahead.

Richard: I know that there are people who are going to read this book and say they don't know Christ, but they want to. They want to get to experience that.

Well, while you were reading this book, some scriptures were dropped here. Go back and search those scriptures. The other thing I wanted to share with you guys is that while you're on drugs, there is the human side of you, the flesh side of you that starts to get angry at God. So I understand those who don't know Christ because for me, it made it worse that I knew Him while I was stuck in this world of smoking crack. I was angry at God. I was mad at God that He made me this way.

So even if you don't know Christ, I'm telling you I knew Christ, and I was still stuck this way, but Christ didn't make you that way. We are the choices we make because God gave us freedom of choice. I know this now, but back then, where my mind was, it was all confused. So that's showing you the type of world I was in. Did I know that Christ didn't make me that way? No. So for the non-believer, I'm telling you: Christ didn't make you that way. I'm glad you brought that up prior, Jenny.. So what I'm going to do right here is ask our audience to just say these words: "Christ, please come into my life. I want to know who You are. I want to know and experience Your love. I want to know You. Christ, help me. Help my unbelief. Strengthen my faith in You, Lord. I believe in You."

Say this, and believe while saying it. That's all you have to say.

He will enter your heart. He will lead and direct you, and He will correct you too.

God always sends what you need, where you need it. We know that we are not alone because we have God. We know that we're not alone because somebody else out there is experiencing what you're experiencing. By sharing your story of what you're experiencing, you could help somebody else to talk about their experience. Know that we're all not just dying in what we're going through because we're not alone. We could all help each other if we all open up and confess, share what we're experiencing so we can help uplift each other. We hope what we've shared is helpful to you. You know, Jen, I just got a couple of scriptures I'd like to share; they will encourage anyone reading this book. I'm praying in the name of Jesus, through the Holy Spirit, that this would affect the reader's heart. This is how I believe that God wants us to put this in you. So 1st Peter 5:7 says, *"Cast all your anxieties on Him, because He cares for you."* And then Isaiah 41:10 says, *"Don't be afraid, for I'm with you. Don't be discouraged, for I am your God. I will strengthen and help you."*

PSALMS 23:4: *"Even though I walk through the valley, even though I walk through the darkest valley, I will fear no evil, for You are with me. Your rod and staff, comfort me."* And then *Psalms 147:3:* *"He heals the brokenhearted and bandages their wounds."*

That's the kind of God we serve. That's the kind of God that is walking with you right now. That's the kind of God that is securing you and wrapping you in His arms and holding you, letting you know that you're not alone. That's the kind of God that helped us because we weren't alone. Right, Jen?

Jennifer: Yes! We had a married couple in our lives; they weren't alone. They shared their story with us. You know a few folks who shared their story with you, and we were encouraged. So we know we weren't alone even though we felt alone and isolated. And to your point, Rich: We both knew Christ, yet we felt how we felt, and that's probably because for those short moments, we took our eyes off God. I know for me, I've allowed flesh to arise and felt how I felt in that moment. But yet and still, we weren't alone.

Richard: Yep. Looking back on everything, on those struggles, on the journey, it was hard — very hard. BUT GOD.

There were so many things that we didn't even write in the book, moments when God's hand was on us. Our three great children were young at the time, and none of them picked up that generational curse of addiction. Oh, God, hallelujah. I cry tears of joy and celebration. I'm not saying none of it affected our children, but they were shielded from the drugs alone. I celebrate God and thank Him for answering prayers. I just did not want it to latch onto them. Yeah, Jen; they didn't see me, but I would go in the bathroom for about an hour. Thinking about it, guys, God was with us for real.

"I have set the Lord continually before me; Because he is at my right hand, I will not be shaken. Therefore my heart is glad and my glory {my innermost self} rejoices; My body too will dwell {confidently} in safety." — Psalms 16:8–9

CHAPTER 13

FINDING FAITH AND PURPOSE IN RECOVERY

Richard and Jennifer: How faith, spirituality or a higher purpose played a role in our healing journey.

Jennifer: All right, Rich, so all through this book, the one thing I could appreciate is that we did not forget to thank God. We acknowledge Him through it. Even through the good and the not-so-good, we acknowledge Him. And so here we are. How did we find that faith, or how did we maintain that faith and purpose during our recovery periods? How did we do that?

Richard: When you were growing up and you were churched, it's one thing. I was introduced to Christ at a young age, and I was at church because I just was taught to be.

So I was just churched, and it was basic. I'm not knocking it — I don't want anyone to read this book and get offended — but it was basic for me. I had the basics, and through my teenage years, I had men around me that would say things. I had an uncle, whose favorite scripture was, "When I was a child, I thought as a child; when I became a man, I put away childish things." So I was getting little scriptures — "Greater is He that is in me" — I was getting things, and they were being fed to me. I was gaining a better understanding of life and dealing with it. I started getting high as an adolescent, and I threw away my youth. I threw it all away getting high, but there was always something because of what I was born into. I began to grow through the struggle, through the pain.

I could not think through the suffering, and in my life, through those pains, I didn't realize how deep it was. I couldn't see it because I was in a haze. But even through that, even though I was angry at God, I knew that it was God. It's funny. So I was acknowledging that God was there because I was mad at God. After all, God is real and all knowing. Now that I'm thinking about it, I was reacting like if I was mad at my wife. So I was young and growing up in the church, and from then to adolescence, coming into my understanding of things that I was around and then got into, I started moving away from the church.

Knowing what I know now, the enemy got a glimpse of who I was and what was going to be, though other folks may have other ideas. See, that's why you never use your eyes to judge anyone. That's why you never use your eyes on what is in front of you. Faith is the substance of things hoped for and the things that are not seen. That's faith. To those people who judged me, saying I wouldn't be nothing, saying our marriage wouldn't work: Ha-ha. How you like us now? Sorry, I had to put that in there. It's not me bragging about us. I just praise God because He was the God that was in me all those years. Nobody saw it, like I said earlier. Nobody saw when I was crying out to God.

Nobody saw me calling on God. "Help me. Help me. I don't want to be like this."

That demon had a stronghold on me, but my faith was the God in me. The God in me was steady fighting. Remember, we wrestle not against flesh and blood, but against the powers of the wicked and the rules of the air, and God fights our battle. So knowing what I know now, Jen, I can see where, through the stretching and the pulling, God was working. It took a long time. Just like the Israel children wandering the desert for 40 years, it took a long time. I didn't ever think this was going to happen, babe. But you know, even though I agree with you — because I too want to believe that I was churched — what I also believe is that somewhere deep down, even though you may feel like you probably weren't all the way there, we had that faith and that belief.

So even when I had my weak moments — when I was sad, mad, angry or emotional, when I felt like hurting myself and just ending it because nothing had happened, nothing was changing — I still believed. Even the days when I surrendered to God, when I should have left it all there but then went and picked stuff back up, I still believed. I still had faith that God was going to do this. What I didn't know was when He was going to do it, how He was going to do it. I wanted it to happen quickly, fast, in a hurry. You know, I had a whole idea of what I wanted to look like. I didn't know what plan God had, but I believed God, and as I moved away from being churched and started developing a true relationship, things changed. I'm not saying I didn't have a relationship with God when I was churched, but I felt like I was just performing a routine: going to church, joining this, doing that. I was just going, just trying to be faithful the best way I could, but I wasn't working on developing a tight relationship with God, like He is my homie. I wasn't doing that.

Jennifer: Having this experience has made my faith stronger. It has made me stronger. There are stories in the Bible that talk about sufferings people went through, like Job, for instance. They had to go through these things to come out stronger, and so this happened. Some may say it didn't have to happen, but it happened. The important question was: Was I willing to go through the process? So I went through the process, and I was iffy with my faith. I was wavering, because I still operated in my natural eye. To be honest, it was hard to see my husband that way and to feel what I was feeling. My natural eye was seeing that, and then when I got away from my natural eye, I just leaned back on God again. So it was like it felt like a flip-flop, a teeter-totter. But I still had faith. I still believed. I had hope. Richard: But you said something, though. You said that people may say that it shouldn't have happened, but again, some scriptures prove that God knew me before I was in my mother's womb. If God knew me before I was in my mother's womb, God knew what I was going to go through.

So with us going through this, through the journey of drug addiction, through the pulling and the tearing and the ripping and the crying and the anger — and sometimes, for me, the hate for people because I was just tired of hearing stuff and knowing that the people who claim to love God were the very ones gossiping —to God again be the glory. He knew the plan He had for me, and it was a plan for my health, for me to prosper and to have a bright future. So when we moved to my recovery stage, I surrendered everything to God and began to, as you said, crave a relationship. Some of y'all practice religion. It's about having a relationship with God. And I began to make it personal because I had to be grateful to my God for what He took us from, for what He brought us out of. I had to be grateful, and I owed a lot to him. There is a song that we sing, "All to Jesus I surrender..." Give it all to Him. He deserves the highest of my praise. He deserves the highest of my gratitude." That's how I began to pour in, and I began to pour out so that he could get it, he could see it. He could see how grateful I was. And as I was pouring out to Him my gratitude and my praise, He began to steadily pour blessings into us — blessings upon blessings upon blessings.

Jennifer: But you know what, Richard? We always heard this. I've always heard this, and I've begun to believe it truly. In our experience, no matter what the enemy sets up for evil or for his bad ways, God always gets the glory. Amen, amen, amen. And so we lived through that turmoil, we went through that disaster, we went through that pain, that hurt, that everything. Even after everything the enemy put on us and kept putting on us, look at God today.

Richard: What the devil meant for bad, God turned it for good. To God be the glory. We're beginning to praise God right now, for Him giving you victory through your storm. Hallelujah, yes. Hallelujah, yes. Hallelujah. Thank You, God, for giving victory to that person who's being set free right now.

And so God had a purpose. He turned this; that's what we

experienced. He turned things for His own good, like we said, right? Because look at us today. This is the first time we're telling our story or our experience in this manner, and this much of it. But we have told it in pieces and patches here, there, in front of the church, little testimonies. Our story has been out to affect lives, not for us but to celebrate, to boast about what God has done. And so now we are telling it more in-depth. Of course, in this book, you're probably still not going to get all of it, but you're going to get a huge chunk of it. We couldn't have done this without God — I wouldn't even want to. I don't even want to pause and wonder if I could start with me if I didn't know God. What would that look like if I didn't ... I can't even think.

What would it look like if I didn't know God, if you didn't believe that God exists, you know? But we believed. I would be either dead or in jail. Jenny wouldn't have been here. She probably would have been somewhere else, maybe even sitting in the crazy house. There's another saying, and I liked it when I first heard it. It can't remember who I heard it from, but it was some kind of Bishop. It goes, "I'm taking my stuff back that the devil stole from me. I'm taking it all back." I like to say this because when I heard it, I was like, *Oh, I love that*, and it's not biblical — it's just me. And if you can't respect my feelings, I don't know what to tell you. If the devil had his hand on that stuff, he could keep it. I want all new things of God. I want better. If the devil had his hand on it, let him keep it.

Jennifer: And so we didn't find faith. We always had it; we just didn't exercise it effectively.

We didn't fully understand our purpose, but now we do.

Recovery came, and I want to say it keeps on going. It keeps on going, and God is just so beautiful in this experience. God is not done yet. He's not done yet. We shared with our coach that I prayed to God to give me a husband who was free from drugs, a good father to his kids, who would take care of the home, lead the home and love me as a wife. I prayed for those things, and God gave me that answer. I cannot even begin to describe the man that you may be reading about in this book, where God took him from and where he's at today. I cannot begin to describe how God gave me what I didn't ask for. There's also a scripture in the Bible to support that. This is how God works. And so, with the faith that we developed more soundly, God continues to bless us, mold us and shape us. We appreciate God. We appreciate Him. We appreciate this experience we had. Did we like it? No. Were we comfortable with it? No, but we appreciate it because God gets the victory all the time.

Richard: I just wanted to correct my baby — your story will be edited by God. God gave her what she wanted and more. He gave her what she wanted and more. I didn't want to speak on her behalf because she's giving me my flowers. The crazy thing is, I didn't have to pray. I had already prayed for what I wanted in a wife, and God transformed that to match who He made me to be every time I elevated, every time I moved up, even when I was in the gutter. My wife was praying, and God began to elevate me back into my position. My wife knew her position, and God positioned her to accept what He was doing. I want you guys to remember that the road to recovery is a road. Life is a war, so we're not ashamed to tell you we won this particular battle. That's why we're able to talk about it — when you win a battle, you are supposed to be proud that you won it, and you describe what it took for you to win that battle. We're on this journey, and it's a road we have to take. Like Jenny said, we went through something. We went through it, and we keep on moving, and we keep on moving. You never stop moving. You never stop pushing through. We know that life is going to give us more bumps. We're going to have to battle things in our life.

We know that. But what we've learned and what we have developed over time, through the pulling and the stretching and the suffering and all the pains, is that that when we face battles, we're not facing them alone. We have a God who goes before us. He's our banner; He's our high tower. He's your banner; He's your high tower, so you will come through this. God will bring you through this. That's why in this chapter, you're hearing our praise, you're hearing our dedication. This is not about Rich and Jen; this book is to make sure that the focus is on God. We are using our lives as a testimony to point someone to what it takes to overcome a battle, whether it be addiction, pornography, alcoholism, gambling, money spending, whatever it is that's pulling you away from your partner and, most importantly, from God. You have to draw back. That's what the enemy wants; his design is to rob, kill, steal, and destroy.

Jennifer: I just want to say my last thing, hon. While you were speaking, this came to me: Today, as we look at the world, we see a lot of people getting married for the wrong reasons. A lot of people are getting married today, then divorced next week or two days later. So I want to encourage you to cherish marriage. It takes work. Don't just look from the outside into someone else's marriage. It takes work, and you have to be willing to be committed. When going into marriage, going in for the long haul, don't be so quick to give up. Don't be so quick to throw in the towel. If you have God in it and let God lead it, then there will be no concern. The stuff will still exist — the pain, the whatever, will still be there — but you know that the outcome is going to be dynamic because God is involved.

CHAPTER 14

Early Days of Recovery

Richard and Jennifer.: Practical advice for couples going through similar struggles — communication, boundaries and support networks

Although drug addiction can be a deeply challenging issue within a marriage and within families as a whole, by focusing on healthy communication, setting clear boundaries and building strong support networks, couples and families can work together. We're not experts in this — although one would argue that we are because we've dealt with the experience. There is no one-size-fits-all solution. Having stated that, we would like to use this opportunity to share or to inspire others. We'll use this chapter to encourage and support couples.

The intensity of the drug addiction was not immediately apparent to us, especially Jennifer. However as time went on, the changes became pertinent. Things can go downhill quickly, so take it seriously. Ask for support, and keep seeking help no matter what.

Be honest and transparent: Both partners should commit to having honest communication about the addiction, the recovery process and any challenges that arise. Avoid hiding or downplaying issues, as this can create mistrust. Don't hold back, and be mindful not to play the blame game.

Look to God for direction. Look for programs for therapy and rehabilitation. Consult your pastor. Be in the company of positive people. Avoid being alone. Be honest with yourself and the people you select to share what's happening in your marriage.

We understand that it could seem more difficult than it is, but guess what? We were solitary for a while. We didn't immediately ask for assistance. We thought we could have completed this process on our own. I, being Richard's wife, believed that I could have helped my husband without anyone. I believed I was strong enough to handle it on my own, and I believed that I could take care of my man. We now know that whatever action he would have taken, good or bad, he would have had to make that decision for himself, and I would have had to accept it as his wife. I would have had to trust God, and there it was — it all worked out for the goodness of the Lord.

We both felt ashamed of all the difficulties we were dealing with one way or another, and who could we really trust at the time? However, we encourage you not to do what we did. Seek help and support as soon as signs arise.

We're aware that it is not always easy; however, we persevered through these difficult times we had. Continue to pray. If you're unfamiliar with Jesus, get to know Him and learn more about Him. In times of weakness, He is a tremendous source of strength. Surround yourself with fellow believers. Participate in church services, read the Bible, pray to God and ask for guidance, forgiveness, grace and strength.

Being near the brokenhearted is discussed in Psalms 34:17–18, while Philippians 4:13 reminds us that we are strengthened by Christ and can accomplish anything. There are numerous redemption stories in the Bible; you're not by yourself.

We're here to share our experience because yes, it has been occurring and is happening to many different couples and families out there. Our journey wasn't simple; it was a difficult time in our lives. The emotional and mental strain was sufficient, and carrying it was quite a burden. It's a lot to bear for one person, the person in the marriage that is not addicted to drugs. We don't mean to minimize what you're experiencing, but as Richard's wife, I too was ashamed. Seeing my other half disappearing before my eyes, knowing that people were looking and whispering, was not a good feeling. Although I cried for my husband until I couldn't anymore, some of the tears were for myself. I was feeling dumb, wondering why I was still in that mess.

We understand that seeing your loved ones suffer is painful for you and that it puts stress on your relationship. You must find a place of forgiveness and gather your strength so that you can help your spouse. It sounds simple — we know it isn't. Simply, you are letting go of whatever grip the experience may be holding on you, just letting go of everything that may be bothering you as you watch your spouse fail. It will help you get ready for the future God has planned for both of you.

For the addicted person — be it crack, alcohol or whatever it may be — you're not in control. We challenge you to look at your spouse. See the hurt, see the shame, see the tears, see the anger and see the trust she had in you diminishing. Know that this is what you're causing because you've chosen the addiction over your spouse. Remember your vows when you tell your spouse you love them and that you'll be what they need. In the addiction, you're no longer what you said you would be in your vows. Take this challenge: Write out your feelings. Exchange what you wrote with each other. Maybe go into different rooms and read it. Release and let God lead. Be open with each other; honor the little victories. Have faith in the impending transformation.

All the while, you establish boundaries that promote respect and healing for both of you, which is crucial for your emotional and mental well-being.

Deal with it head-on, don't put it off and don't be afraid of the outcome. God is a God of grace and mercy, so even though it may feel uncomfortable, you're moving towards the beginning of healing.

Don't let this process take you out. God is in the middle; see Him and believe.

Though we're not sure what your situation might be, we're urging you to persevere. It may take a different method and entail more layers. Grab hold of a Bible and get into Psalm 129, which will encourage and equip you. Read the book of Proverbs, which is meat for your soul. Our only goal is to encourage, inspire and bring hope to you. Because God is dependable, there is hope for your circumstances. Go seek God and all of His righteousness. He is dependable; He has been continuously faithful and will forever be faithful until the end.

We know He can do for you what He did for us. God can accomplish anything, even if it doesn't look the same or have the same result. We hope this inspires you, gives you hope and helps you along the way because God can accomplish anything. Rebuilding a marriage after addiction is possible with God, patience, resilience, commitment and willingness to grow together. Remember the power of God's grace and surrender your struggles to God, trusting that His power is made perfect in our weaknesses. Lean on Him and trust Him to take you through the process; He is the ultimate source of hope and strength (Corinthians 12:9 NIV).

We stand in the gap on your behalf. We give thanks to God for every couple in the world, for every couple who might be going through something. We don't know what level it is, where they are or what's going on in their marriage, but whatever it is, we give it to You, and we pray that You will uplift, sustain and restore in the name of Jesus. Lord, You said in your Word (Psalm 41:3 ESV) that You sustain them, Father. We pray they would reach out to You, dear God. Thank You, God, that they will listen to You and do what You say in advance. On his sickbed, in his illness You restore him to full health. Father, nothing is too big for You to handle, and we believe that You will do what You've promised them.

God, lead them to the right people on their path, and send them to the right places for support. Strengthen them in the name of Jesus. God, You give power to the faint, and to him who has no might You increase strength (Isaiah 40:29 ESV). God, You were our source, and we believe You to be a source for them as well. We pray that they will trust You, dear God, and if they don't already know You, Jesus, we pray that they will learn about You, who is eternal life and our resource. Therefore we give thanks to God for every marriage and family, we condemn the spirit of drug misuse and we declare that the families have been delivered and healed. Lord, You said (in Psalm 147:3 ESV) that You heal the brokenhearted and bind up their wounds. So Lord, we thank You in advance for the healing.

We ask you to execute in their lives the blessings You have for them, guide their feet and open the eyes of their heart, and that they would have a listening ear to each other and work together in this process with You at the forefront. It's under Your matchless name that we give thanks to God and express our gratitude for the support, inspiration, grace and mercy You have shown us and will show them. Thank You for providing the family with strength. We also want to thank You for curing them and for providing them insight, and dear God, we thank You for saving us and saving them; In Jesus name; Amen.

CONCLUSION

Richard and Jennifer: A final reflection on how far we've come, the importance of ongoing healing and the hope we have for the future

This structure allows both husband and wife to share their unique perspectives while highlighting the emotional and relational complexities of battling addiction together. Each section would offer practical insights for readers who are walking a similar path.

Richard
If the things you are struggling with are causing damage to your relationship with God and your family, then take a good look at yourself.

You may find that the cause is you.

If you feel convicted, don't take it as a bad thing. All it means is that the Holy Spirit is at work. Let the Holy Spirit do its job. Become humble; know that your suffering will produce something great.

People are going to count you out, and even that is okay. Stay the course. Your journey is for you to travel, not for other people. You will be able to see God strengthen you in your weakness. Give up on yourself, and believe in yourself (inner self). Catch that — *believe inner self.*

You will see things start to change. No one wants to hear that they're wrong or even feel that they're are wrong, but sometimes you have to come to the realization that you have done wrong and ask for forgiveness. Go to people you offended, apologize and ask for forgiveness. You're going to be all right. I'm a witness. It takes time, but the outcome is that you will have peace and joy. There's nothing better than that.

Be who God called you to be. Stay blessed. I love you. More importantly, God loves you.

Jennifer
Looking back on our journey together, I'm struck by how far we've come. It's clear that healing isn't about reaching a final destination — it's about learning to embrace the process. I was an enabler in many ways, and that realization was mind-boggling, but I had to own it. This was a tough process, and by no means did I want to go through it, but I had to for whatever reason. This journey of unlocking who we are, processing what we experienced, healing what was broken and restoring what was lost is ongoing.

The distance that grew between us during the painful moments was the same distance that allowed us to gain strength and faith. It allowed the healing to begin. There were countless nights when I thought I'd lose him, and honestly, I felt like giving up at times, but I couldn't bring myself to. The recovery process has been humbling. There's been joy, but there's also been pain and slip-ups — and the power of resilience lives on. I used to sometimes hide what I was truly feeling from Rich because I was fearful of disagreements, and that pushed him to want to leave the house and go find his drug buddies.

Each step has been a reminder of the damage addiction caused and how it had the power to break our marriage to a point where it seemed unsalvageable — but there is hope for everyone, and all things are possible with God if you only believe. Through the hard work of recovery, I've learned that healing is ongoing, and I'm grateful for the chance to rebuild our lives together. Loving someone with an addiction is lonely, and I often felt like I was fighting alone, but I held onto my faith and my belief that we could come through this if we kept pushing forward, even when I didn't have all the answers. Healing, for me, has also meant forgiving not just him but myself for the times when

I thought the worst of myself and him. It's been a journey to rebuild trust, to redefine what love and partnership mean in a way that acknowledges the past but doesn't allow me to stay in the past. Every day is a choice, a decision to love and to grow together. We're stronger, and our bond is more honest than ever. Our journey is far from over, but our hope is unbreakable. We're committed to nurturing a relationship where we continue to heal, laugh and hold each other through life's highs and lows. If I could share only one message, it's that recovery and healing are not isolated paths but intertwined journeys. I hope others know that they too are capable of breaking through, one day at a time, and finding light on the other side.

You are stronger than you realize. Through the chaos of addiction and recovery, you have the power to find healing —

for both of you. Unlock what's on the inside.

"*² And if I have the gift of prophecy [and speak a new message from God to the people], and understand all mysteries, and [possess] all knowledge; and if I have all [sufficient] faith so that I can remove mountains, but do not have love [reaching out to others], I am nothing. ³ If I give all my possessions to feed the poor, and if I surrender my body [a]to be burned, but do not have love, it does me no good at all. ⁴ Love endures with patience and serenity, love is kind and thoughtful, and is not jealous or envious; love does not brag and is not proud or arrogant. ⁵ It is not rude; it is not self-seeking, it is not provoked [nor overly sensitive and easily angered]; it does not take into account a wrong endured. ⁶ It does not rejoice at injustice, but rejoices with the truth [when right and truth prevail]. ⁷ Love bears all things [regardless of what comes], believes all things [looking for the best in each one], hopes all things [remaining steadfast during difficult times], endures all things [without weakening]."* — *1 Corinthians 13:2–7*

FINAL MESSAGE FROM US

Through our story, we've shared the pain, the doubts and the struggles. But more importantly, we've transparently shared the hope that transformation is possible. NEVER DOUBT GOD! Brokenness doesn't have to define you, and healing doesn't mean forgetting what happened. It's simple: Find strength in your story, learn from your experiences and please allow God to weave beauty and love out of your broken places.

ABOUT THE AUTHORS

Richard and Jennifer Kinard are a devoted husband-and-wife team who have turned their trials into triumphs, sharing a message of hope, faith, and restoration. With over 31 years of marriage, they have weathered the storms of addiction, separation, and broken trust, emerging stronger and more committed to one another and their faith.

Richard is a father, grandfather, plumber, and skilled handyman with a passion for helping others rebuild their lives. Known for his resilience, wisdom, and unwavering faith, he uses his life experiences to encourage others on their journey toward healing and redemption.

Jennifer is a compassionate educator, mentor, and author who brings her creative spirit and nurturing heart to every role she fulfills. As a mother and grandmother, she has a deep understanding of the importance of family and the power of grace. Her work reflects her commitment to guiding others toward restoration and growth, offering inspiration through her words and actions.

Together, the Kinards are living proof that love, faith, and determination can overcome even the darkest of challenges. Their book, Broken Together Healed, is a raw and uplifting account of their journey through addiction and recovery, offering practical insights, personal reflections, and spiritual encouragement for couples and individuals facing similar struggles.

Beyond their writing, the Kinards enjoy serving others, organizing, watching movies, and spending time with their family. With a shared passion for inspiring others, they are dedicated to showing that no matter how broken life may seem, God's love and grace can lead to healing and renewal.

Other Works by Jennifer Kinard:
- The Journey
- El Viage (Spanish version of The Journey)
- Nothing But Gratitude: A Journal

Richard and Jennifer are honored to share their journey, believing that every broken person can be restored through faith, perseverance, and the transformative power of God.

www.ingramcontent.com/pod-product-compliance
Lightning Source LLC
Chambersburg PA
CBHW030453100526
44580CB00009B/114/J